AF291451

Here is a body. It is oils. It is a browning of the ages.
It is beauty, full. It has a trap door.

Here are the bodies. They are shaped of curves and juts.
They have extended their wings limbs to be seen far and wide:
an alterable terrain. They are possessed in the margin seeking
visible invisibility.

See an eye. See how it glints and cuts. Sight of even fields
collating the endless visions of many. Who will see her? Tangibly
she sees with (her) touch what she cares to take in the most.
The rest she uses her eyes for: adrift. Through windows of contempt
a multitude passes her: displaced. This land is big enough for
all of us, yet, totems can be both ladder, periscope and structure.
I think of the twenty-seven tears the years have wept me. Reality
is an eyesore to be birthed from. Outside of eye, I don't know.
With those eyes…

See hands, see feet. Feet met foot: a pounded path carrying
care, sourced from the psyche of the knowing unaccepted.
Hands met hold fast: carved from labour cut from escape routes
should they be needed again. Here lie the rivers, the roads,
the trails, the ridges, the bridges, the paths, the streets, the steps,
the pavements—paved for weather, pounded for her use. All life
I've walked abroad in London. Hands wringing writing from
scorched earth. Wrote mourning to me, wrought meaning to me,
meaning: tender foot step back awhile in case my breast should
leak a dust, crippled, speak. Pink from pressure rising in the east
and settling in the west, can she arrive now she has landed?
'Who will take her place if a space is made?' they say. 'For someone
has to be on the bottom—sorry at the rear—sorry at the back,
breaking work would labour hear my plea or are they busy
painting the red with blues?'

See lungs. Lungs of incapacity of capacity for incapacity. Opacity
means breath unseized, for the world claims colour of the air so
no regions for brown breath only brown lungs are you worthy.
How she breathes? Slowly. Muscles loosen away from bone where
nothing is mine, mine fault, mine duty, mine drive… mine,
is only the loosening of you all and the loosening of me. On to be
a truly loose freed woman at one with all she has lost. How she
breathes? How she breathes is how she holds her breath. In the
fumes known poisonous to the human. Those positioned lesser are
submitted to its cloud. Here she holds her breath to help hold her

tongue when the homeless in the earth's eye misting early hour
call for her change she cannot spare and sings in languages formally
used to colonise 'nigger' this or 'negroid' thats.

See soul. Soul bearing fruits of weighted spirits speaking
through her, holding through her; wings apart. At full span spun
from concentric circles, of unholy duppies dem a members
could easily be called fraud, absence and impossibility, but here,
lie in her being as once imaginary, thrice symbolic and only real.
Where in her body lies her soul? Where in her body lies your
soul—you who places yourself in her mother's mouth, claims all
the paths she attempts to take, perforates all the windows her
privacy cowers within, blocks all the ways to breathe dreams into
tomorrow. Am I depressed? Are you impressed? Hold fast a cake
will soon come with candles leaking wax into the ears of those
who could carry your wish away from this place, this reading, this
weeping, yet sung movements are all we have and every time
I enact mine my limbs remember they can always echo instead.
Just that little bit more, just that shift of weight and out damned
spot new faith. With I as saviour and we as chorus to ride upon.

See the end of the world as we know it: yes, see the place in between.
See the womb. See the breasts. See the vagina. See the reproduction.
See the Atlas. See worlds that only begin at a black woman's tale.
Splayed out and heavy-like. Where broken in the birth, a system
that sees us just like horses. Birthed in the broken bereft of a seat to
hold her. More seat-shaped from her, back, depressed, lifting
islands of new nations birthed from her broken tongue lingering
languages lapped from the shores of those who are the true other that
we landed in. On my arrival, I ask you to see that which you
choose to shun. I now choose new plains to shield from. The margin
is a greatness possible to yield a self-controlled environment ever
framed by my eye: our eye: she, seeking invisible visibilities.

See mouth. Mouth pursed, pressed, parted, plucked; pronounced.
How does her speech hold the air off of candlelight? Lip-locked
turns to tongue-locked, turns to teeth ground down and out, down
and out. Instead, breaaaaaaathe breath. Instead, hope the world
comes crashing down on your lip overhang by pronounced oppression.
Wet of salvation, saliva blind me for I may have better hold
of a sense of speech, a sense of depth of fields sewn not trodden, yet,
I can feel the footprints on my back as I 'yeah' and 'fair' the day's
pain away. Mouth measures the moves and sings of charged disdain.
Shout, mouth, shout; yet, held mouth hold.

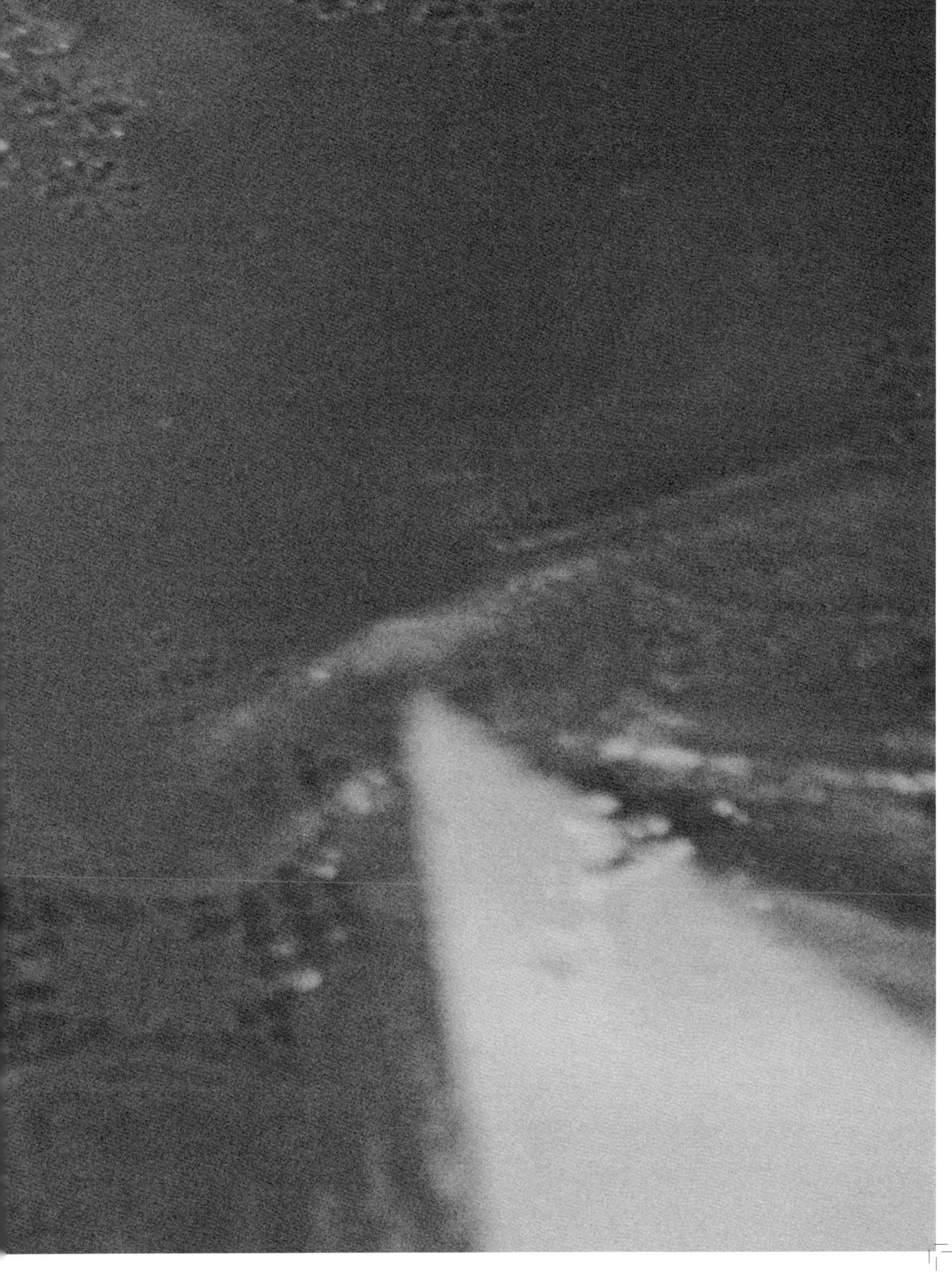

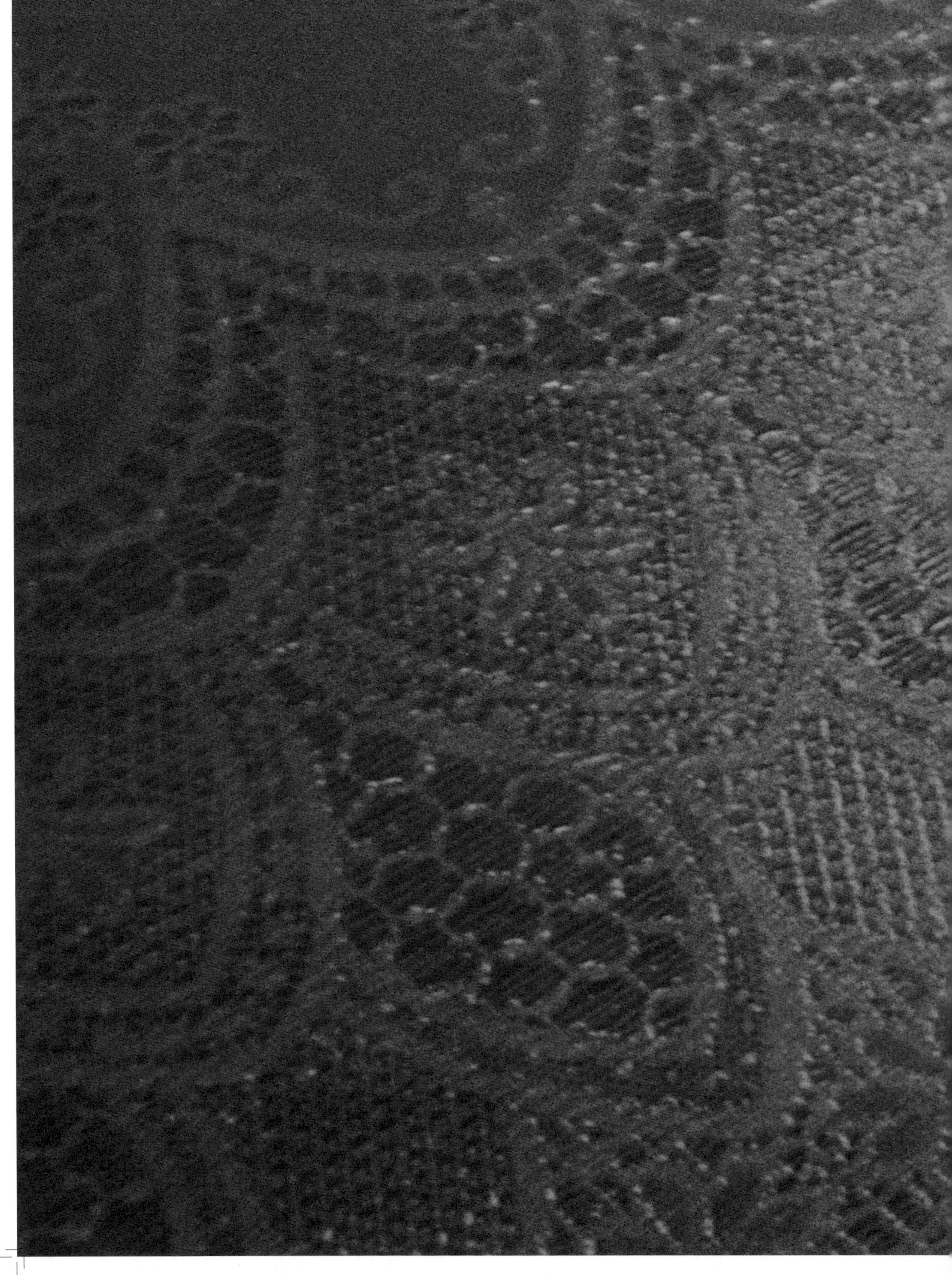

See an eye. See how it glints and cuts. Sight of even fields
collating the endless visions of many. Who will see her?
Tangibly she sees with (her) touch what she cares to take in the
most. The rest she uses her eyes for: adrift. Through windows
of contempt a multitude passes her: displaced. How are the
women of the first island different from the women of my second
(island)? It feels like they busy the idea of themselves less.
Blouse and skirt makes sense as surprise, as through clothed
eyes all can be seen. This land is big enough for all of us,
yet, totems can be both ladder, periscope and structure. I think
of the twenty-seven tears the years have wept me. Reality
is an eyesore to be birthed from. Outside of eye, I don't know.
With those eyes…

I

BARBARA FERLAND

EYES

AT THE UNIVERSITY

AT THE UNIVERSITY

MY friend, the calabash grows beside the lectur-
    er's window,
Leaning an untrained ear towards the tutored din,
Bemused, relaxed, — its stout roots shaded;
Tosses mute shadows on the walls within.

WHISTLING a wind-tune. Bounces a dancing
    seed
Against its uninstructed gourd;
Twirls the ball of its shape in the round hand of
    the wind—
Rubs its green thumbs on the chalk-smeared board.

TWICE scarlet gowns, by ten start shaking
    Making
Black mounds of unskinned yams
Above a red-earth field.
Beat
Your disciplined tongue
On the tight drum of your mouth, O white man.
They will not come.
They will not heed.

MY friend, the calabash,
    Grows beside the lecturer's window.

Barbara Ferland

The Sunday Gleaner, March 13, 1960.

EXPECT NO TURBULENCE

Expect no turbulence, although you hold me fast,
For this, where late my love lay, beats no more,
Confute, perplex not; only shield me from the past,
What might have been is lost, not gone before.

Though in the night your surgent need impels
Your body to seek comfort, bruising me awake,
I will not shrink, though all your flesh repels;
Nor sanctuary deny, while we communion take.

For we, two lost, two hungry souls, will meet
At common board, with common need for bread.
You, in the wood, will gather berries sweet;
I, in the dark, taste the salt flesh of the dead.

*See hands, see feet. Feet met foot: a pounded path carrying
care, sourced from the psyche of the knowing unaccepted. Hands
met hold fast: carved from labour cut from escape routes should
they be needed again. Here lie the rivers, the roads, the trails,
the ridges, the bridges, the paths, the streets, the steps, the
pavements—paved for weather, pounded for her use. All life
I've walked abroad in London. Hands wringing writing from
scorched earth. Wrote mourning to me, wrought meaning to me,
meaning: tender foot step back awhile in case my breast should
leak a dust, crippled, speak. She used to clean the church to
support my chance of a better higher education. In the evenings
after work, or on Saturday mornings, she would join the other
browning women to clean up. After the sinners have been
cleansed and the heavens rejoiced—with bleach in her teeth
in her throat she would clean/clear the way for me to meet a
godly path of worthy advancement and scholastic achievement.
Pink from pressure rising in the east and settling in the west,
can she arrive now she has landed? 'Who will take her place if
a space is made?' they say. 'For someone has to be on the bottom
—sorry at the rear—sorry at the back, breaking work would
labour hear my plea or are they busy painting the red with blues?'*

II

ZOÉ SAMUDZI

HANDS & FEET

HEAVY HANDS WEATHER

Work itself is not romantic, but there is poetry
in its motion – in her motion. Even as her presence/
arrival was a result of a trans-generational crossing
of waters, her movements and her musculature, steady
and deliberate, radiate. There's nothing romantic
about the work itself, there's nothing spectacularly
praiseworthy about her labour: the consequence
of centuries of coercions, displacements, extractions
and exploitations. Because in order to serve *her* family,
she's forced to abandon her own. All of the air in
her lungs is expended in order to ensure some other
child is fat, fed and cared for.

The nucleus of this ecology of work and sweat
is breath. Breath is, at once, part of a global ecology
and our individuated 'ontological dependence on
air and its implications for [those of us] whose lives
rely on the continuous material exchange with our
surrounding gaseous environment.'[1] The air that fills
and empties from her lungs, an autonomic inhalation
and exhalation exchanging oxygen and carbon
dioxide, is an intake and expulsion of an atmospheric
anti-blackness. This atmosphere 'trans*forms'
and weathers black being through a climate whose
transnational meteorological conditions are oriented
towards and around black death.[2] In this economy
of exhaustion[3] – a vampiric political economy whose
transformations and technological advancements

iii

are always predicated upon the maintenance of an
underclass of racialized labourers – she is worked
and *over*worked (as though the border between the two
is ever clear). The mechanics of her working movement
are always retracing circuitries of extracted labour
that preceded her and anticipating the ones that will
inevitably follow. Her labouring body is situated
within a formulation of purely corporeal black selfhood
without interiority: a body-[non]mind suited only
for work, and whose 'materiality is thought to provide
the observable "fact" of animality,' a femaleness
attached to her labour as a beast of burden contra to the
paradigmatic white feminine womanhood to which she
is tethered as a subordinate.[4]

She is black because she works,
  she works because she is black.

No matter where she is – whether the Caribbean or
the necro/metropole; the far flung equatorial native zone;
or the civilised imperial core – her working presence
is made material through the so-called 'Old World's'
battering ram collision and collapse into the 'New'.

***

iv

Circulations, chiasmatic recursivities and routes
between crime scenes on both sides of the Atlantic
bring her labour[ed] movements to scale. Triangular
trade as a transnational cartography of her drudgery:
her everyday/every day responsibilities, her quiet
suffering, a routine entanglement of fragmented
black being foundational to the machinations of white
life. In human anatomy, 'chiasm' is the place where
two biological structures (whether tendons or nerve
fibres) cross and form an x-shape, the Greek letter *chi*;
it connotes crossover and exchange. This crossing is a
racial co-constitution: a chromatic 'mutual implication
of conventional opposites – subject and object, mind
and body, viewer and viewed, eye and hand'[5] mapping
onto a constantly reiterated black/white colour line.
'The moment of contact between two hands' – the
constantly moving hands doing work and making life,
constitutive of her labouring body – 'is a defining
condition of being in the world.'[6]

While Elizabeth Abel's concept of the affective wrinkle
originated with respect to the photograph, it can
be readily appropriated to the phenomenology of her
working body; the grooves of raced-gendered labour
hewed into her flesh. The wrinkle makes way for
an 'affective overflow'[7]: the ridged disruption when
you unsmooth a piece of fabric, a politic of refusal
in which life is made and remade even as it is fated

v

to robotic demands to work. An interracial proximity
between herself and whomever conscripted her labour.
The wrinkles formed by, stitching together, her flesh
is evidence of the 'fact of blackness'[8] – the product of
a sociogeny and a racialising gaze that affixes morality
and social hierarchy onto the body via an epidermal
racial schema.

She is black because she works,
  she works because she is black.

Even as she's whole and embodied, she's reduced
to a spectre – at once indispensable and absent. A home
may fall into disrepair and disorder without her,
but hers is a labour that nevertheless goes unrecognised
because any and all gestures towards her personhood
are displaced by her person as synecdochical with
labour's value-form. Always, and, thus far, only ever
existent within a genealogy of chattelisation.

***

vi

This international of expropriated labour leaves
no one whole, no one intact. The severed hands
of native workers in the Congo comprise their own
cartographies of imperial and postcolonial extraction.
The working parts – limbs and reproductive
organs – are more valuable than the so-called
persons they constitute.

There is 'no pathway to her thoughts, no glimpse
of the vulnerability of her face or of what looking
at such a face might demand.'[9] She is equal parts
imagined here and ubiquitous, the wrinkle extends
into a fabulatable haptic gesture that refuses the
sole spectacle of racial abjection. Maybe we consider
her contemplative prayer.

Did she ever, when she clasped those working hands
together, rebuke the Lord in the way his faithful
servant Job would never? Did her feet shift; did she
fall to her knees; did she clasp her hands in mournful
lamentation; did she hold hands with or embrace
another? Whether she prayed or wished or cursed; did
she know both how much and how little would change?

She is black because she works,
  she works because she is black.

vii

1 Caterina Albano, *Out of Breath: Vulnerability of Air in Contemporary Art*, Minneapolis 2022.

2 Christina Sharpe, *In the Wake: On Blackness and Being*, Durham 2016.

3 Françoise Vergès, 'Capitalocene, Waste, Race, and Gender', *e-flux*, no.100, May 2019 (https://www.e-flux.com/journal/100/269165/capitalocene-waste-race-and-gender/), last accessed 9 May 2023.

4 Zakiyyah Iman Jackson, *Becoming Human: Matter and Meaning in an Antiblack World*, New York 2020.

5 Maurice Merleau-Ponty, 'The Intertwining — the Chiasm' in *The Merleau-Ponty Reader*, eds. Ted Toadvine and Leonard Lawlor, Evanston, Illinois 2007.

6 Elizabeth Abel, 'Skin, Flesh, and the Affective Wrinkles of Civil Rights Photography' in *Feeling Photography*, eds. Elspeth H. Brown and Thy Phu, Durham 2014.

7 Ibid.

8 Frantz Fanon, *Black Skin, White Masks*, New York 1967.

9 Saidiya Hartman, 'Venus in Two Acts' in *Small Axe*, vol. 12, no.2, summer 2008, pp. 1–14.

See lungs. Lungs of incapacity of capacity for incapacity.
Opacity means breath unseized, for the world claims colour of
the air so no regions for brown breath only brown lungs are you
worthy. How she breathes? Slowly. Muscles loosen away from
bone where nothing is mine, mine fault, mine duty, mine drive…
mine, is only the loosening of you all and the loosening of me.
On to be a truly loose freed woman at one with all she has lost.
How she breathes? Because of yoga I have a hypersensitivity to
my breath whenever I approach a task. That task could be putting
pen to paper or that task could be releasing stress by releasing
my bowels. I listen intensely to the sound of air travelling through
my nostrils, through my ears by the fairest (in thickness never
in colour) hairs that cloak my limbs. I marry the auditory
experience. How she breathes is how she holds her breath. In the
fumes known poisonous to the human. Those positioned lesser
are submitted to its cloud. Here she holds her breath to help hold
her tongue when the homeless in the earth's eye misting early
hour call for her change she cannot spare and sings in languages
formally used to colonise 'nigger' this or 'negroid' thats.

III

FRANÇOISE VERGÈS

LUNGS

BREATHE TO RESIST

NOTES ON A QUEER, BLACK, INDIGENOUS AND BROWN FEMINIST MOVEMENT

This is the summary of a speech that retold the birth
of the 'Breathe to Resist' feminist queer movement
during its first planetary meeting. Indeed, in 2074,
hundreds of women, trans and queer people, coming
from different parts of the globe, finally met in a secret
place in East Asia because they had to hide from
the private militia and armies of the global racial
capitalist dictatorship that took hold by the late 2040s.

In the 2040s, as scientists had foreseen, the
consequences of racial politics and the economy
of unbreathing became obvious. Centuries of racial
capitalism had fabricated an irrespirable planet,
literally. Unbreathing not only meant the increase
of asthma, respiratory diseases, or lung cancer
that made black, indigenous and brown people more
vulncrable to premature death, but also an increase
of authoritarian regimes that curbed joy, speech and
dissent. 'Suffocating', which expressed the feeling
of being strangled, was soon a reality. A majority
of black, indigenous and brown peoples were born with
non-full-lungs that greatly hindered their capacity
to breathe and to survive. As a result of the lack
of oxygen, rivers, forests, lakes, animals, birds, plants
and fish started to die. The fascistic parties, which
dominated states, were too busy chasing and killing
refugees, black, trans and queer people, to take
care of communities. They denied the problem and
diffused fake news – blaming leftist groups, refugees,
trans and queer people for bringing viruses and
diseases that would explain the rise of incapacitated
lungs, rather than listening to the World Health
Organisation's warnings.

iii

Already in the 2020s, the WHO had insisted
the threats on individuals' health were created by
air pollution and contamination caused by racial
capitalism's extraction and exploitation. This was
mostly among poor and racialised communities
worldwide: more non-white babies were born with
respiratory diseases, 7 million premature deaths
annually, 2.4 billion people exposed to dangerous
levels of household air pollution and 39.7% of babies
were stillbirths. For a while there was traffic for
oxygen bottles, but most people could not afford to
buy them and therefore watched their children and
close ones dying of suffocation. Rich, white people
appropriated the production of oxygen: living
in domes with trees, flowers and birds, protected
by heavily armed mercenaries and soldiers who
arrested, tortured, imprisoned and killed anyone
who studied ways to produce oxygen. In this economy
of suffocation, people were worked to death,
which was usually in their early thirties. Restricted
lungs meant that people could not sing and scream.
They had to be very careful with breathing and often,
in order to get through the day and night, they
learned to hold their breath, accelerating the time
towards their death. The air they breathed was thick
with toxic fumes, entering every corner of their
houses and darkening them with grime. Food was
not only scarce, but had the taste of dust. There were
no birds, no trees, no flowers; their world had the
colour of ashes. Premature death became a given.

However, in the late 2050s, in different parts of the
world (first in a township of Durban, in poor villages

iv

and neighbourhoods of Port-au-Prince, in the northeast
of India, the Rif Mountains, in Louisiana, and
Guatemala), some women were born with lungs capable
of filtering heavily polluted air; giving them the ability
to breath, whilst giving birth to girls with a similar
capacity. They turned to indigenous science and African
diasporic knowledge to cultivate plants that produced
oxygen even in heavily polluted environments
(yet unknown to scientists). Upon this knowledge they
developed a cure that not only enhanced their lungs'
capacities, but allowed their offspring to be born
with full and healthy lungs. The 'Breathe to Resist'
movement was born, founded by black, indigenous
and brown women, trans and queer people in 2058.

The group organised an underground network
which slowly became planetary. They devised ways
to communicate practice and knowledge. At the
beginning, they understood that by breathing
repeatedly into the mouth of a person, they could
prolong the life of non-full-lung peoples. They soon
realised that this was too long, laborious and they
could not save many lives this way. They learned
techniques to slowly build back damaged lungs and to
amass oxygen. They could not remain underground,
they had to create places where they would produce
clean air and clean water, cultivate plants, bring
back birds, insects and butterflies protected from
the armies and mercenaries. The first communes
reached out to each other to exchange knowledge
and experiences. They consulted elderly black,
indigenous and brown women, women in Africa
and the Arab world who knew how to create oases

v

with little water, which in turn would facilitate
the growth of plants and trees that produce oxygen.
Young women were sent on long journeys from
one commune to the other to collect knowledge, seeds
and testimonies. The 'Breathe to Resist' movement
also organised the defence of their communes, first by
establishing them far from the fortresses where rich
whites were living, by borrowing from old tactics of
maroon communities and anticolonial movements, then
from indigenous weaponry–hiding a commune behind
trees and plants, settling on top of a mountain to see the
enemy coming, learning to blend into the landscape or
using the landscape as a weapon. Within two generations,
they had built underground refuges and sanctuaries
where people could find a place to escape enslavement
and to repair their lungs, as well as farms where
they could grow plants, food and flowers. Arriving in
a 'Breathe to Resist' space was a wonder: butterflies,
birds, plants, flowers, children singing and playing, the
sound of clear voices... Early on they decided to deal
with the irreparable: some plants, trees, animals, birds
and fish would not come back and some people would
not recover from damaged lungs. Though those that
did were attended with tenderness and love, and new
species of flowers and plants were discovered and
cultivated. They knew that depriving people of air had
a long history: captives lacking air and strangled in the
slave ship, black people shocked to death by police,
polluted industries built near poor and racialised
communities. In the twenty-first century, 'I can't
breathe' had been a global rallying cry against police
violence and the afterlives of slavery and colonialism.
'We breathe' was theirs.

vi

The notes taken from the speech end there. But as I
read them in 2080, in the library of a 'Breathe to Resist'
community, I understand how important it is to know
that history. If it were not for these women, queer and
trans feminist peoples, the enslavement of non-full-lung
people would have gone unchallenged. We know their
names, we cherish their memories, we seek to live
up to their commitment. Our network has grown since.
The struggle to fight against the privatisation of air by
the wealthy and to make breathing an equal right
for all has mobilised people around the planet. Our
scientists and laboratories work for the communities.
We have developed a philosophy based on the right to
breathe as the founding element of social organisation.
We have communised everything. The future is ours.

*See soul. Soul bearing fruits of weighted spirits speaking through
her, holding through her; wings apart. At full span spun
from concentric circles, of unholy duppies dem a members could
easily be called fraud, absence and impossibility, but here, lie
in her being as once imaginary, thrice symbolic and only real.
Innately fragmented. Comparable to colonisation's presence in
the makeup of Caribbean identity inherited by the New World-
generated descendents. Did you know Britain is the successful
Old World meeting New World? They don't know what to do
with themselves caught in the loop of a fascist comfort. Turned
round yet not turned around; the 'a' represents a turning of mind
versus a turning of cheek. The ships went one way, years later
another voyage with planes too, thus, on a round to finish a shape
of trio concerto etched as the only known known of an unknown
known fragmented by slavery of where (and when) is (was) home.
Where in her body lies her soul? Where in her body lies your soul
– you who places yourself in her mother's mouth, claims all
the paths she attempts to take, perforates all the windows her
privacy cowers within, blocks all the ways to breathe dreams
into tomorrow. Am I depressed? Are you impressed? Hold fast
a cake will soon come with candles leaking wax into the ears
of those who could carry your wish away from this place, this
reading, this weeping, yet sung movements are all we have
and every time I enact mine my limbs remember they can always
echo instead. Just that little bit more, just that shift of weight
and out damned spot new faith. With I as saviour and we as
chorus to ride upon.*

IV

VANESSA ONWUEMEZI

SOUL

STRANGER TO THE COLD

That mirror to the world. That reflection
of a reflection folding inwards towards
a bottomless depth. That formless animation
as breath sighs through the lungs, sighs
through the leaves of the plant or the palm
falls to the ground   dies and rots as fruit.

The breath of the spirit transmuted to flesh
whose movement felt but never articulated?
The primary essence   the seat of being?

The protector and dependent.   The tunnel
through the ages opens out of me so that the
ancestors can enter a world that has thrived on
their labour, so that they may find their life,
their freedom.

The stone walls that stand firm around me,
she built. And I shrink into her dark corners,
her aches, her sorrows and losses, her pride,
her triumph, her brick that stands tall holding
the roof raised to the heavens spite the rain,
the rotted window frames I live   I go on.
It is both my home and my furnishing.

iii

The soul. It is   it is? The site of relation
between time and the Outside of time.
The centre around which we turn, around
we turn and our bodies live out the turns
of time here on earth.

My soul. Who took the land as her body
and so rooted there, felt uprooting as death.
Goodbye island. The rupture leaves a
phantom limb, her weight shifts, the body
leans awkward into the void between the
land left behind and that towards which she
moved. And the rootless soul risked being
withered by the journey, but the motherland
promised new soil. So many uprootings,
the soul bears the imprint every time the roots
are left to wither in the sun, they harden.

iv

Harden in the heat, like the burn of the
ground hardened my feet moving over land.
My resolve hardened over the sea as I come,
here I am. Here I am on the red bank of
the Niger, in Western Africa   here
I am in the fields of Bihari, here   I am
in the streets of Hong Kong   mountains
of Guangdong where it rains the thick rain
of the islands, and I breathe out the heavy
vapour that saturates the tangled forests of
Jamaica and tears ran down the rivers
of Trinidad, Antigua as they filled the ships
with flesh, fresh soul, a thousand souls
homebound, one day, for Britain.

And the journey split her one body to new
body. Limb from limb torn into two. The real
and a phantom island veiled forevermore
behind the warm folds of the waves that ushered
away the time, sailing away   goodbye
sharp of the sand, tall of the palm, seed
and stench of the jackfruit, goodbye bodies
and minds broken and reformed. I am, she
is divided limb from limb. 'Bone of bone,
flesh of flesh'[1] emerging from the dark air
she floats in silence across the void, stranger
to the cold, 'you can't go home again.'[2]

v

We are bound to time. 'Created by
destruction'[3], a self split into two and my
soul   my centre is?   Between two
islands, a double life – speaking once but twice,
my reflection in the mirror, in the water, twice
removed. I wake in the morning to two suns
out of sync, two homes, each of my children
born twice and their phantoms walking
the earth, strangers to each other and the life
I left but the life that *I am* knows that these
British city walls, these are the walls that I built.

They were built with my aches, my sorrows
and losses, my pride, my intellect, my roof
raised to the heavens. Carpeting the hallways
is the skin of my feet, like a runner that rolls
over the ground from my home, through
the dark morning hours before the city rises,
to the office block, the school, these sites
of relation my phantom moves and her gloved
hands trace the dirt, the movement of your
hands that have touched but never touch me.
I wipe it away, and rest in the confusion
of your benevolence we are confused, we are
bound to time.

vi

My centre is   dark as the belly of the ship
that bore me once, twice in the port by
the yachts, at the foot of this tower where the
fluorescent lights never dim but shine right
through me a phantom of your and my own
imagination. My hands press palm to palm,
shall I pray to your God?

I can pray because   I love. I can smile
at you showing   teeth for holding in the
tongue teeth for cutting rope. Showing feet
for stamping and praise for walking the
reddening earth rough nylon as the light lows
and darkness of night knows intimately that
eternal darkness which is home, the house of
the soul. So say Black. Black forged from two
worlds and the void between them, melting
together in a furnace of suffering and to desire
it is my becoming. I can't go home again.

So I built this city brick by brick. I drew my
energy from the wind at the top of the tower,
and the strength of the waves that move forever
through my body's memory. I drew my steam
from the heat at my centre and my centre
forever burns, my centre, my soul, is One.

vii

1   W.E.B. Du Bois, 'The Souls of Black Folk' in *Writings*, New York 1986, p.360.

2   Stuart Hall, *Essential Essays, Volume 2: Identity and Diaspora*, Durham & London 2019, p.194.

3   Gaiutra Bahadur, *Coolie Woman: The Odyssey of Indenture*, Chicago 2014, p.63.

*See the end of the world as we know it: yes, see the place
in between. See the womb. See the breasts. See the vagina.
See the reproduction. See the Atlas. See worlds that only begin at
a black woman's tale. Splayed out and heavy-like. Where broken
in the birth, a system that sees us just like horses. 'Save your
tears, blood is more useful here'. Birthed in the broken bereft of
a seat to hold her. More seat-shaped from her, back, depressed,
lifting islands of new nations birthed from her broken tongue
lingering languages lapped from the shores of those who are the
true other that we landed in. Gendered: she, is here and has
always split back open to bear fruit of all labours. I've known
a she subsumed as he to disregard ideas of alterable terrain.
On my arrival, I ask you to see that which you choose to shun.
I now choose new plains to shield from. Not yet skin (tight), not yet
killer (roach), not yet local blood (mosquito), not yet grown (roots),
instead full of poisonous nature(s), yet present. The margin
is a greatness possible to yield a self controlled environment ever
framed by my eye: our eye: she, seeking invisible visibilities.*

V

KATHERINE MCKITTRICK

WOMB, BREASTS
& VAGINA

INTEGERS & AGONY & DISCORDANCE

BLACK WOMEN ARE THE MECHANICS OF SLAVERY

Demonic Grounds, 2006

THE WHITE STUDENT WAS AROUSED BY DESSA ROSE'S SCARS,
SO I LEFT THE CLASSROOM AND DIDN'T RETURN FOR WEEKS

Black Feminist Thought Seminar, Winter 2008

I WANT TO FORGET THIS... HOW CAN I FORGET THIS?
I DON'T WANT IT ANYMORE

Worn Out, 2017 [1]

In Reckoning with Slavery, Jennifer L. Morgan presents various numbers
that account for, and count, captured black men, women and children.
The numbers and numberings are endless, specific and opaque: '36, 110
voyages; the trade in trinkets; 152 captives, gold, male and female slaves;
a group of enslaved Africans; the layout of a slave ship; 725 enslaved
persons... mostly women.'[2]

Morgan draws attention to how these numbers function as evidentiary
texts, or social facts, that also obfuscate the gendered dimensions
of enslavement.

The numbers, calcified by economic interest (accumulation of wealth,
accumulation of more enslaved workers, accumulation of free labour,
accumulation of bourgeoise subjectivity) illuminate what cannot be counted
(black women's robust presence and their participation as the collective
(non-consensual) fulcrum of slavery; their affective labour; their physiological
labour; their social and sexual reproduction; their sense of place; and
their subversive and rebellious acts, plus, terror).

Morgan's *Reckoning with Slavery* provides a meaningful entry into
histories of black femininity, black corporeal worlds, and black geographies;
her study threads demographic and economic specificity (the selling
of the enslaved and related profit-making processes) to activities that cannot
be easily deciphered (extra-numerical and extra-economic processes).
The pairing of archived data with unevidenced histories offers an unresolved
contradiction that situates the black feminine body (the black feminine,
black womanhood, the black mother, the black worker, the black caregiver)
as vaguely – yet still – accountable.

It follows that the black feminine body cannot simply be conceptualised
as an enfleshed-knowable-object. It follows that the black feminine is not,
a priori, enveloped in negativity and fungibility across time and space.
Then and within the living memory of slavery something else is swirling.

v

In fact, if the body and integers and accountability unravel as contradictions, rather than ahistorical-knowable-objects, a conceptual space is pried open, one that brings into focus black feminist embodied agency. Embodied agency, the physiological and creative and intellectual work of black women's livingness, is the act of living otherwise and creating worlds and rebelling against systems of domination, all of which are humanising practices that undermine plantocratic and colonial representations of black femininity. Or, the static and negative and fungible image (e.g. enfleshed-knowable-object, numerically concretised) is ruptured by embodied activities that are uncertain and unpredictable and world-making. Or (again), crude conceptualisations of the black body are both thrown into relief and undone by the presence of *and* conceptualisation of agentive black feminine embodiments – activities that are propelled by humanising praxes that expose the alterability of the black corporeal terrain.

The contradiction between the data and the unevidenced (here so many of us dwell, forever, it seems) elicits how the black enslaved body (the fulcrum of slavery, she/they who non-consensually advance rapacious accumulation through violence) cannot (should not) be conceptualised as object (data, datum, unit, commodity) precisely because this legitimises (resolves, verifies, normalises) numeric architectures of white supremacy that are, in fact, *made discordant* by black women's wilful reimagining of what their body can do and is. Here, lightening fast, we switch from centering the body, we question the analytical preoccupation with the black feminine/female body and two-sexed systems, and we bring into focus a range of gendered and feminine embodiments; opaque, legible, vague and everything and everywhere, all threaded to, but not defined by the damaging integer.

For the black scholar, the body alone elicits incredible pain; to conceptually anchor everything and everywhere to black feminine flesh (to glue theoretical scaffolding to her/our/their pained body). For the black scholar, body parts (womb, breast, vagina) are sites of extraction (real and conceptual/ 'they took my milk').[3]

Discordance is perhaps a mode of repair.

vi

How is this done? The installations of Rhea Dillon provide a visual pathway
that both tracks and reconfigures the corporeal brutalities that accompany
plantation slavery and its aftermath. We are tasked to enter – walk within,
move around – structures that suture black femininity (womb, birthplace,
between the legs) to extra-human objects (atlas, gourd, altar, spine of ship).

Dillon's pulling apart of black womanhood is a reminder
of plantocratic and colonial practices:

black women came to be increasingly appraised for their fertility/
in the eyes of slaveholders/
slave women were not mothers at all/
they were simply instruments guaranteeing the growth
of the slave labor force/
their monetary value could be precisely calculated/
in terms of their ability to multiply their numbers.[4]

The pulling apart requires knotted contradictions (the precise calculations,
the un-mothering, the guarantee, the monetary value and the appraisal).
And it brings into sharp focus the plantocratic functions of black femininity
(the fertility, the womb, the broken womb, the future labour force and
the spine of ship) as entangled with a global economy. Put otherwise,
as she is violently torn apart and assessed, her productive and reproductive
labour accumulates wealth for those empowered by racial capitalism,
transnationally (cotton, tobacco, rice, sugar, and more and more opulence).
Dillon provides a trace of these economies – not integers but traces –
and wraps them around black femininity through naming and incongruous
pairings and repetition: womb/atlas captures and unframes gourd/birth/
drink/alter/slave ship/womb. Lessons crop up: the atlas is/as womb, fills
up the world; atlas is/as book of maps, is/as globe, is/as cartography,
is/as navigational tool, is/as maritime log. Or: the atlas and the womb give
us the grammar to name the legible (precisely calculated) and opaque
(not mothers at all) as paired (and repeated) modes of unresolved reparation
that function to illuminate how the living memory of slavery (violence,
accumulation, opulence, global markets) requires but cannot totally define
black femininity. Or: agonising discordance.

vii

1   All quotations Katherine McKittrick.

2   Jennifer L. Morgan, *Reckoning with Slavery: Gender, Kinship, and Capitalism in the Early Black Atlantic*, Durham 2021, pp.31, 81, 49, 129, 237, 152, 192.

3   Deirdre Cooper Owens, *Medical Bondage: Race, Gender, and the Origins of American Gynecology*, Athens 2017; Sara Clarke Kaplan, *The Black Reproductive: Unfree Labor and Insurgent Motherhood*, Minneapolis 2021; Toni Morrison, *Beloved*, New York 1987, p.20.

4   This is a reconfiguration of Angela Davis, *Women, Race and Class*, New York 1981, p.7.

See mouth. Mouth pursed, pressed, parted, plucked;
pronounced. How does her speech hold the air off of candlelight?
Lip-locked turns to tongue-locked, turns to teeth ground
down and out, down and out. Instead, breaaaaaaathe breath.
Instead, hope the world comes crashing down on your lip
overhang by pronounced oppression. Wet of salvation, saliva
blind me for I may have better hold of a sense of speech,
a sense of depth of fields sewn not trodden, yet, I can feel the
footprints on my back as I 'yeah' and 'fair' the day's pain
away. Mouth measures the moves and sings of charged disdain.
Shout, mouth, shout; yet, held mouth hold. The woman
in me grieves for syllables I lost in youth.

VI

MARTINE SYMS

MOUTH

MOUF

MOUF

Diaphragm exercises

Sitting at the edge of a chair with your feet firmly on the ground inhale through your nose deeply, to check on this you will feel the pressure of your butocks on the chair. Remember to loosen up your neck and shoulders.

1. Release the air as if you were blowing a candle (use your finger in front of your mouth to keep the reference).
2. Release the air with a controlled "S" sound.
3. Release the air loosely with a soft "F" sound.

Repeat each exercise at least 5 times.

The aim of this exercise is to tone the diaphragm muscle so keep the same pressure from beginning to end without arcs. A constant and controlled stream of air.

Dear Rhea,

READ THE FOLLOWING ALOUD:

"They pounded the walls with their fists, finding a shared and steady rhythm that they hoped might topple the cottage, make the walls crumble, smash the cots, destroy the reformatory so that it would never be capable of holding another 'innocent girl in the jailhouse.' [...] Almost every window of the cottage was crowded with Negro women who were shouting, angry, and laughing hysterically." [1]

A SONIC PROTEST

MOUF

Dear Rhea,

~~Dear Rhea,~~

READ THE FOLLOWING ALOUD:

Diaphragm exercises

Sitting at the edge of a chair with your feet firmly on the ground inhale through your nose deeply, to check on this you will feel the pressure of your buttocks on the chair. Remember to loosen up your neck and shoulders ~~you can't move~~

1. Release the air as if you were blowing a candle (use your finger in front of your mouth to keep the reference).
2. Release the air with a controlled "S" sound.
3. Release the air loosely with a soft "F" sound.

Repeat each exercise at least 5 times.

The aim of this exercise is to tone the diaphragm muscle so keep the same pressure from beginning to end without arcs. A constant and controlled stream of air.

"Where the activity of the voice and all
my openness to the way the voices of
Trouble
and Future enact
In their huffing and distortion the possibilities
inherent in human presence in sounds /
that middle range of intelligibility where we
walk the earth." [2]

(I fucked up the spacing)

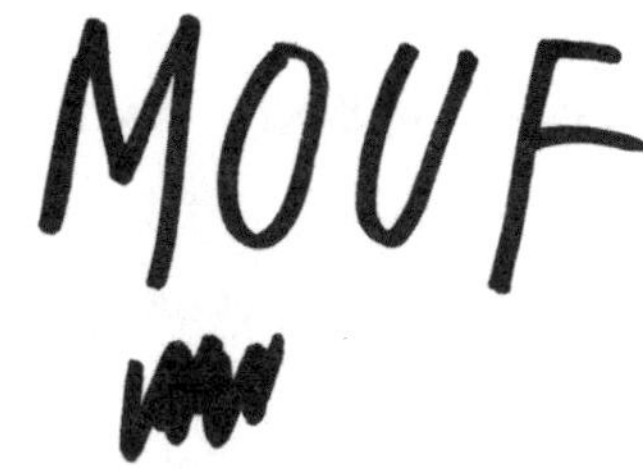

Diaphragm exercises

Sitting at the edge of a chair with your feet firmly on the ground inhale through your nose deeply, to check on this you will feel the pressure of your butocks on the chair. Remember to loosen up your neck and shoulders.

1. Release the air as if you were blowing a candle (use your finger in front of your mouth to keep the reference).
2. Release the air with a controlled "S" sound.
3. Release the air loosely with a soft "F" sound.

Repeat each exercise at least 5 times.

The aim of this exercise is to tone the diaphragm muscle so keep the same pressure from beginning to end without arcs. A constant and controlled stream of air.

You said mouth but I heard voice.

In other words,

one's basic vibration.

Eh (as in whether) — the THROAT

HAM — the throat

Start with a groan. You might want to be alone
After taking a full breath, let the groan begin
at the bottom of your feet. Allow the groan
to take its own direction in its own time,
without thinking about it
If you have to think think of the sound a black hole makes

Laryngeal and Vocal Cord Exercises

These exercises should be completed slowly and with attention to your voice quality. They should be done at as low a volume as you can sustain. Anyone can belt out sounds, but the exercise is in maintaining improved voice quality in your softest register. Have some water close by so you can take sips during these exercises.

1. The Yawn-Sigh: Begin by attempting the most authentic yawn you can imagine. Lift your chin slightly; open the mouth wide so that you feel a stretch in the jaw. Feel your voice box in your throat with your flat hand on your neck. It should go down when you yawn. Pull your tongue back along the floor of the mouth, and breathe in deeply. You may yawn better by stretching your arms and shoulders as one might do in the morning.

2. As you exhale, sigh 'ah' and hold it out for three to five seconds. The voice quality should be soft and cottony as it comes from deep in your throat. Don't allow the voice to turn off mid-way through your sigh. The exercise is in the soft cottony sigh. You should feel really open in your throat. Repeat these yawn-sighs eight to 10 times slowly with attention to the quality of the voice, the accuracy of your form, and the feeling of openness you get.

3. The Fog Horn: Begin with a deep lower abdominal breath (see step one of the warm up on page 1). Purse your lips into a narrow 'O' shape. Make an 'oo' vowel sound (like 'oops') on a low comfortable note and hold for six to eight seconds. Your voice quality should be very quiet and breathy. Relax the cheeks and allow the breath to puff them out. There should be some air flow through your lips (like you would do to make a candle light flicker). If you are doing this exercise properly, you will feel a vibration in your lips or nose. If you don't feel this, try using a lower pitch and more air. Repeat 10 times.

4. The Lip or Tongue Trill: This exercise is similar to the fog horn above. Begin by taking a deep lower abdominal breath. Bring the lips together and jut them out slightly. Make sure your lips and cheeks are relaxed. Begin breathing out as you produce the sound "Brrrr." The lips should trill consistently. If they stop moving or stop trilling, take another breath and begin again. If you have trouble trilling with your lips, try your tongue. Repeat 10 times.

5. The Pitch Slide: Your goal is to slide softly from your lowest pitch to your highest pitch as you say the word "Whoop." Make sure the sound is soft, with lots of breath support and with an extra 'puh' sound at the end of the word. Imagine saying "Whoop-puh." Repeat eight to 10 times, then reverse and slide your pitch from high to low. This time, say the word "boom." Repeat eight to 10 times. In both cases, focus on the sound and vibration at your lips. The goal is to perform the slides without voice breaks.

Another thing I like to do is put on a
drone and sing with it. Odesza Mini taught
me that. 396 Hz is a good frequency

The following exercises are designed to reduce vocal fold and laryngeal tension and increase range of motion, balance between airflow and vocal fold closure and to ease vocal production. If possible, complete one or two times daily (in the morning and in the afternoon or evening). but anything will work.

The musical pitch G corresponds to the throat chakra

1. Take the first two to three minutes stretching your upper body (or if you have time the whole body). Reach up with your arms; try to bring your elbows together in the back. Shake your hands down by your side.
2. Roll your shoulders. Begin first with the left shoulder. Roll it eight to 10 times. Allow the rotations to become larger as it is comfortable to do so. Repeat with the right shoulder. Make the movements slow and easy.
3. Roll your neck with eight to 10 rotations to the right and left. Make these motions slow and sweeping. Start with your chin straight down against your sternum. Think about your chin as a pendulum. Roll your chin over to the right shoulder. Hold this position for a slow count to five. Move your chin back to the middle. Repeat on the left side. Each time you roll, stop in the middle. Hold these positions for a slow count of five. When you do this activity, let your mouth open slightly.
4. Now, take 10 deep breaths into the lower abdomen. Feel your stomach expand; feel your lower back fill with air. Pay careful attention to your chest and neck which should both remain still and flat. Lay a hand on your stomach and one on your chest to feel their movements.
5. As you breathe in, the stomach should move outward. As you breathe out, the stomach should flatten. Remember that breathing is a matter of moving the muscles of the stomach, without tensing the muscles of the chest and shoulders.
6. After the 10 breaths, inhale through the nose or pursed lips then exhale with five easy "S" sounds. After producing "S"switch to "Z". Concentrate on the vibration of your tongue and the roof of your mouth. Make sure your shoulders remain still.
7. Try some easy, exaggerated chewing, like you have a few pieces of bubble gum in your mouth. If necessary, use your hands to massage your cheeks. Chew for two to three minutes without making a sound, then chant or hum while you are chewing. Let your voice come out easily and softly.

Warm - up of the folds: & its balance the fifth above D.

- Mouth closed hum in a lower comfortable range for 3 minutes.
- Mouth closed hum in a lower comfortable range changing the vowels slowly (a-e-i-o-u) for 3 minutes

I sang a G just then for ten minutes

♡ mmmm

1   Saidiya Hartman, *Wayward Lives, Beautiful Experiments: Intimate Histories of Riotous Black Girls, Troublesome Women, and Queer Radicals*, London 2019, p.279.

2   Simone White, 'Sh!t' in *or, on being the other woman*, Durham, North Carolina 2022.

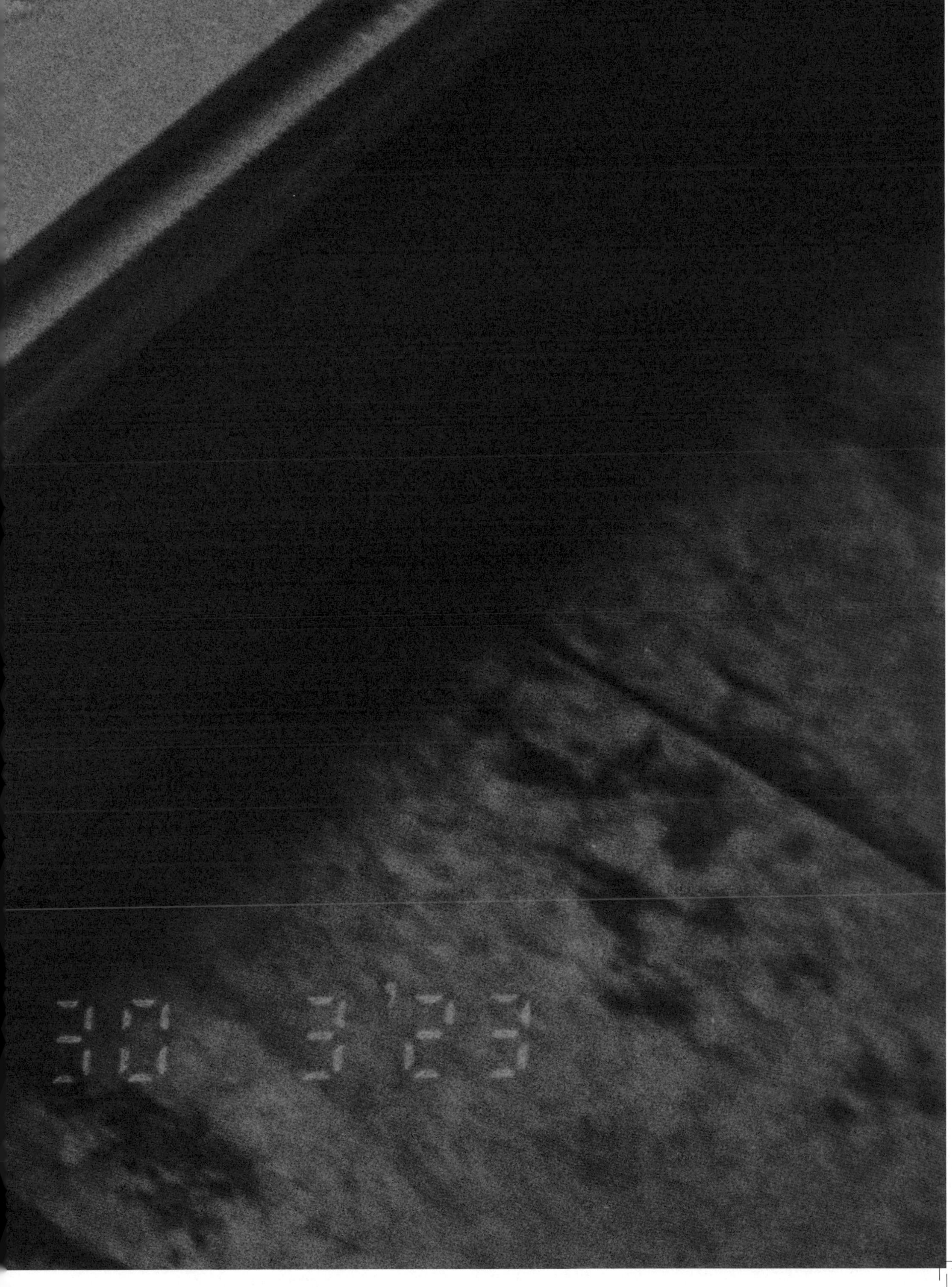

Here is a body. Of what would you describe to make her? It is oils. It is a browning of the ages. It is beauty, full. It has a trap door.

Here are the bodies. They are shaped of curves and juts. They have extended their wings limbs to be seen far and wide: an alterable terrain. They are possessed in the margin seeking visible invisibility.

See an eye. See how it glints and cuts. Sight of even fields collating the endless visions of many. Who will see her? Tangibly she sees with (her) touch what she cares to take in the most. The rest she uses her eyes for: adrift. Through windows of contempt a multitude passes her: displaced. How are the women of the first island different from the women of my second (island)? It feels like they busy the idea of themselves less. Blouse and skirt makes sense as surprise, as through clothed eyes all can be seen. This land is big enough for all of us, yet, totems can be both ladder, periscope and structure. I think of the twenty-seven tears the years have wept me. Reality is an eyesore to be birthed from. Outside of eye, I don't know. With those eyes…

See mouth. Mouth pursed, pressed, parted, plucked; pronounced. How does her speech hold the air off of candlelight? Lip-locked turns to tongue-locked, turns to teeth ground down and out, down and out. Instead, breaaaaaaathe breath. Instead, hope the world comes crashing down on your lip overhang by pronounced oppression. Wet of salvation, saliva blind me for I may have better hold of a sense of speech, a sense of depth of fields sewn not trodden, yet, I can feel the footprints on my back as I 'yeah' and 'fair' the day's pain away. Mouth measures the moves and sings of charged disdain. Shout, mouth, shout; yet, held mouth hold. The woman in me grieves for syllables I lost in youth.

See lungs. Lungs of incapacity of capacity for incapacity. Opacity means breath unseized, for the world claims colour of the air so no regions for brown breath only brown lungs are you worthy. How she breathes? Slowly. Muscles loosen away from bone where nothing is mine, mine fault, mine duty, mine drive… mine, is only the loosening of you all and the loosening of me. On to be a truly loose freed woman at one with all she has lost. How she breathes? Because of yoga I have a hypersensitivity to my breath whenever I approach a task. That task could be putting pen to paper or that task could be releasing stress by releasing my bowels. I listen intensely to the sound of air travelling through my nostrils, through my ears by the fairest (in thickness never in colour) hairs that cloak my limbs. I marry the auditory experience. How she breathes is how she holds her breath. In the fumes known poisonous to the human. Those positioned lesser are submitted to its cloud. Here she holds her breath to help hold her tongue when the homeless in the earth's eye misting early hour call for her change she cannot spare and sings in languages formally used to colonise 'nigger' this or 'negroid' thats.

See hands, see feet. Feet met foot: a pounded path carrying care, sourced from the psyche of the knowing unaccepted. Hands met hold fast: carved from labour cut from escape routes should they be needed again. Here lie the rivers, the roads, the trails, the ridges, the bridges, the paths, the streets, the steps, the pavements – paved for weather, pounded for her use. All life I've walked abroad in London. Hands wringing writing from scorched earth. Wrote mourning to me, wrought meaning to me, meaning: tender foot step back awhile in case my breast should leak a dust, crippled, speak.

She used to clean the church to support my chance of a better higher education. In the evenings after work, or on Saturday mornings, she would join the other browning women to clean up. After the sinners have been cleansed and the heavens rejoiced – with bleach in her teeth in her throat she would clean/clear the way for me to meet a godly path of worthy advancement and scholastic achievement. Pink from pressure rising in the east and settling in the west, can she arrive now she has landed? 'Who will take her place if a space is made?' they say. 'For someone has to be on the bottom – sorry at the rear – sorry at the back, breaking work would labour hear my plea or are they busy painting the red with blues?'

See soul. Soul bearing fruits of weighted spirits speaking through her, holding through her; wings apart. At full span spun from concentric circles, of unholy duppies dem a members could easily be called fraud, absence and impossibility, but here, lie in her being as once imaginary, thrice symbolic and only real. Innately fragmented. Comparable to colonisation's presence in the makeup of Caribbean identity inherited by the New World-generated descendents. Did you know Britain is the successful Old World meeting New World? They don't know what to do with themselves caught in the loop of a fascist comfort. Turned round yet not turned around; the a represents a turning of mind versus a turning of cheek. The ships went one way, years later another voyage with planes too, thus, on a round to finish a shape of trio concerto etched as the only known known of an unknown known fragmented by slavery of where (and when) is (was) home. Where in her body lies her soul? Where in her body lies your soul – you who places yourself in her mother's mouth, claims all the paths she attempts to take, perforates all the windows her privacy cowers within, blocks all the ways to breathe dreams into tomorrow. Am I depressed? Are you impressed? Hold fast a cake will soon come with candles leaking wax into the ears of those who could carry your wish away from this place, this reading, this weeping, yet sung movements are all we have and every time I enact mine my limbs remember they can always echo instead. Just that little bit more, just that shift of weight and out damned spot new faith. With I as saviour and we as chorus to ride upon.

See the end of the world as we know it: yes, see the place in between. See the womb. See the breasts. See the vagina. See the reproduction. See the Atlas. See worlds that only begin at a black woman's tale. Splayed out and heavy-like. Where broken in the birth, a system that sees us just like horses. 'Save your tears, blood is more useful here'. Birthed in the broken bereft of a seat to hold her. More seat shaped from her, back, depressed, lifting islands of new nations birthed from her broken tongue lingering languages lapped from the shores of those who are the true other that we landed in. Gendered: she, is here and has always split back open to bear fruit of all labours. I've known a she subsumed as he to disregard ideas of alterable terrain. On my arrival, I ask you to see that which you choose to shun. I now choose new plains to shield from. Not yet skin (tight), not yet killer (roach), not yet local blood (mosquito), not yet grown (roots), instead full of poisonous nature(s), yet present. The margin is a greatness possible to yield a self controlled environment ever framed by my eye: our eye: she, seeking invisible visibilities.

She, her own alterable terrain.

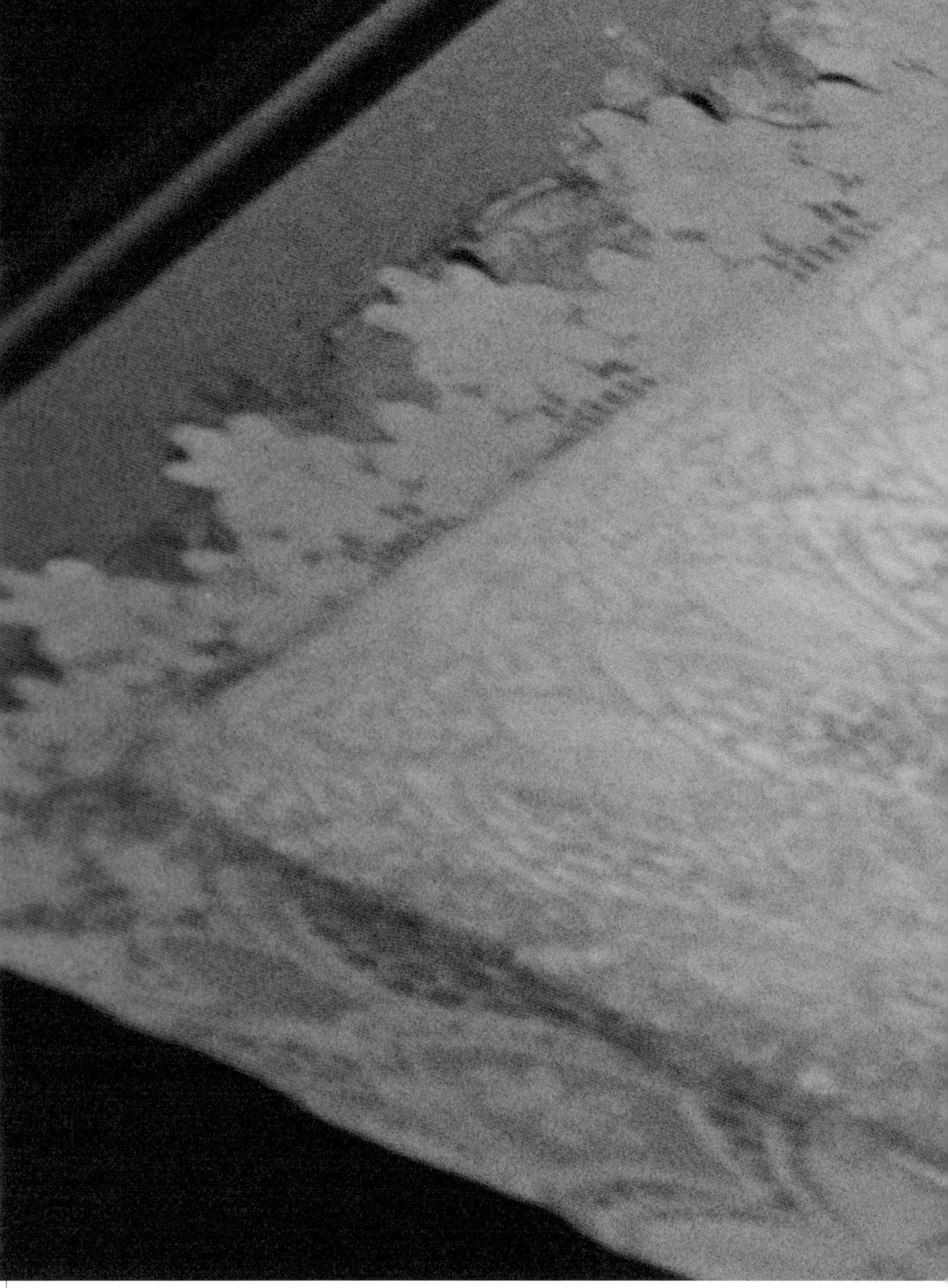

Eyes	*Flagging Visions Of Periphery*, 2023 Steel, polyester and resin, 104.5×130 cm
Mouth	*As Wata to Wine, Wine to Blood, Blood to Dirt, Dirt to Sand, Sand to Water; Wata (Bit)*, 2023 Iron, plastic and sand, 10.2×40.7×30cm
Lungs	*Placing Her Within An Alterable Terrain,* 2023 Acrylic glass, 160×160×160cm
Hands & Feet	*C/leaning Figures,* 2023 Scent, soap, molasses and resin, Dimensions variable
Soul	*An Unholy Trinity (the) Imaginary, Symbolic and Real,* 2022 Sapele mahogany, 117×87×87cm
Womb, Breasts & Vagina	*Swollen, Whole, Broken, Birthed in the Broken; Broken Birthed, Broken, Deficient, Whole—At the Black Womb's Altar, At the Black Woman's Tale,* 2023 Sapele mahogany and calabashes, 25.4×160×25.4cm

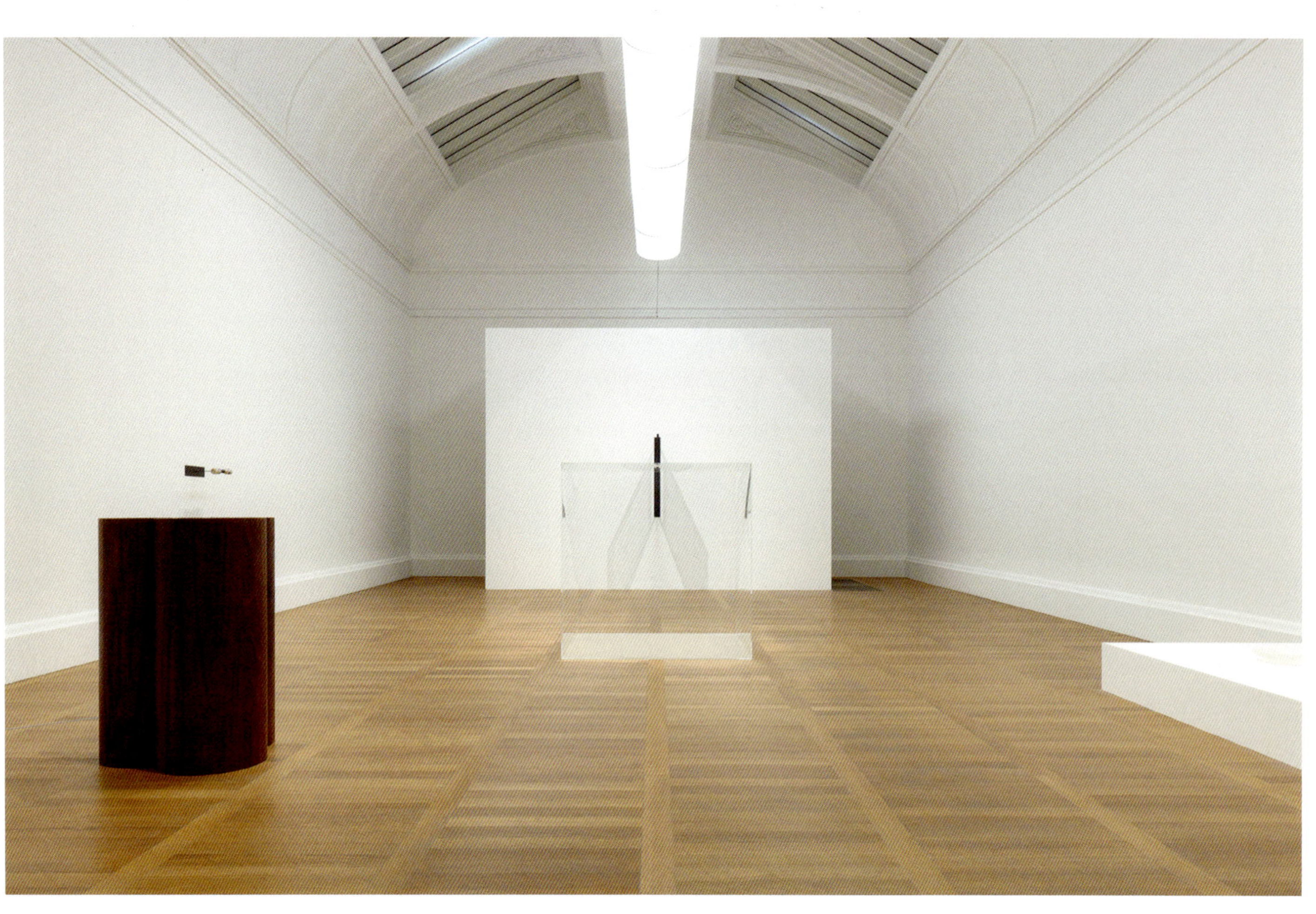

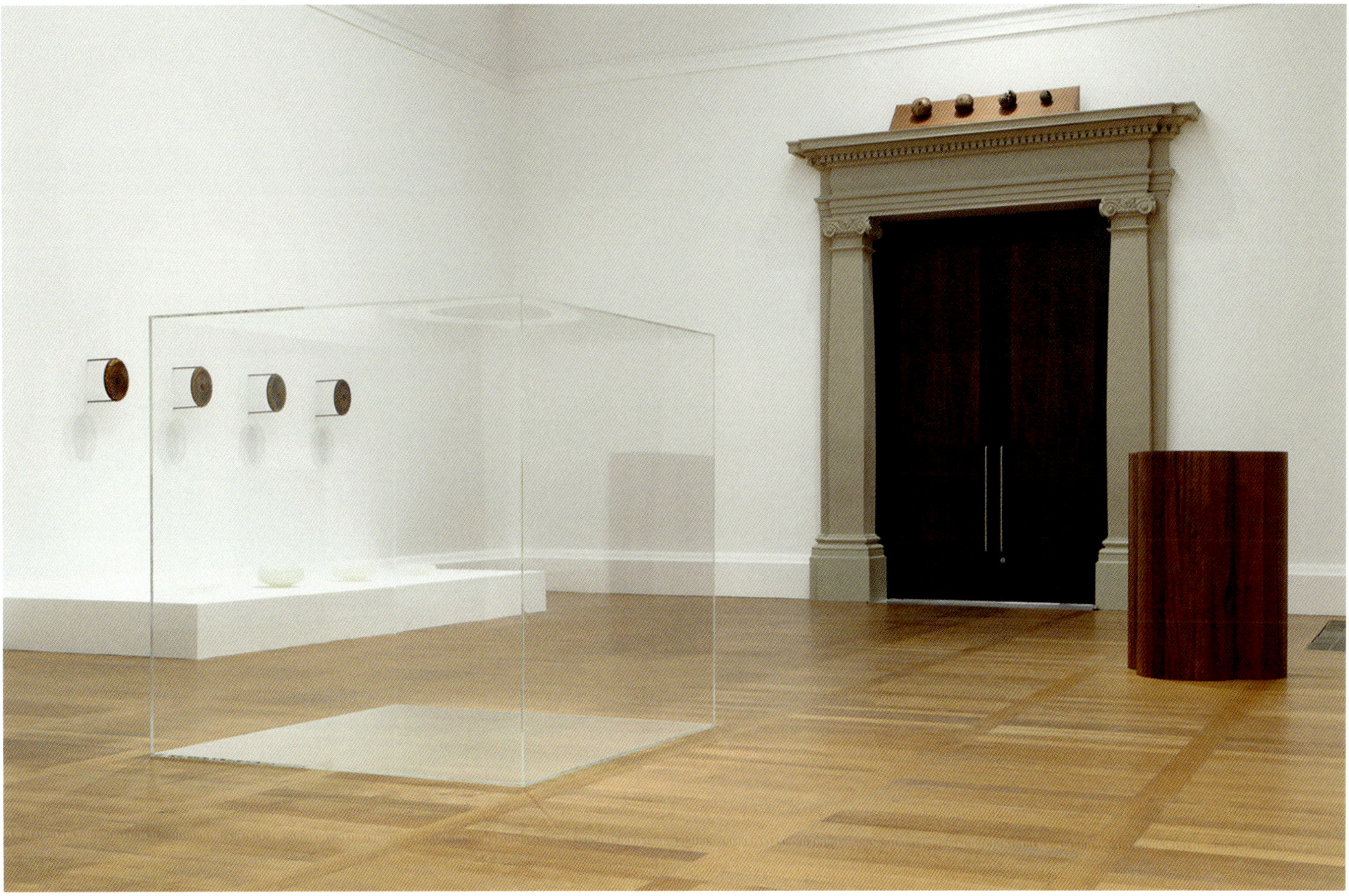

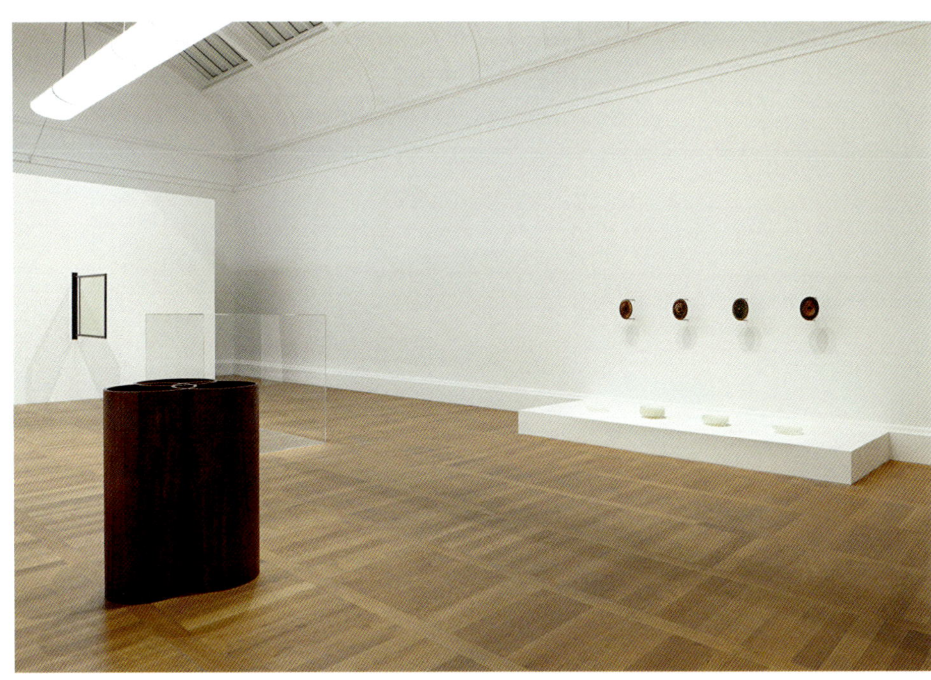

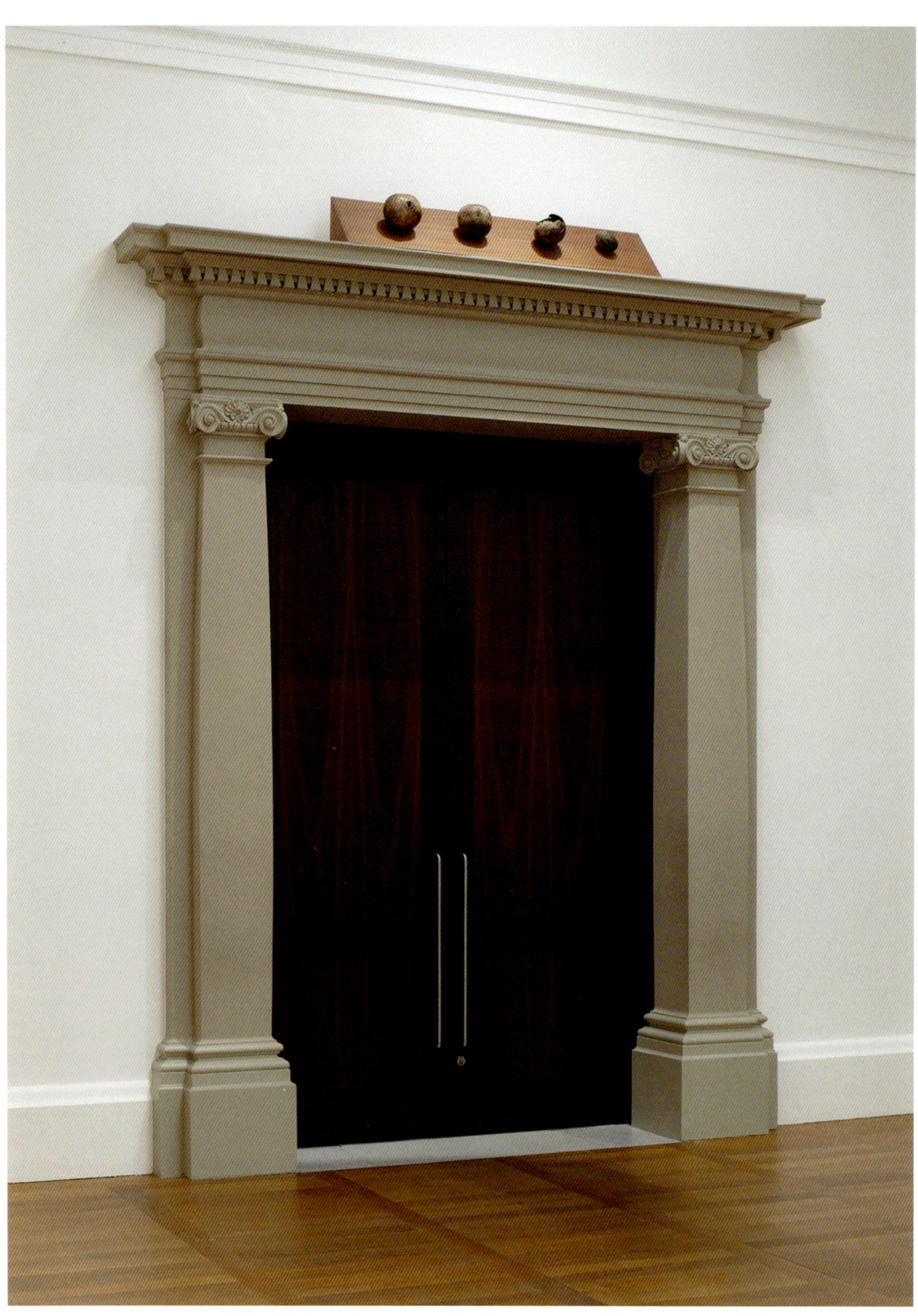

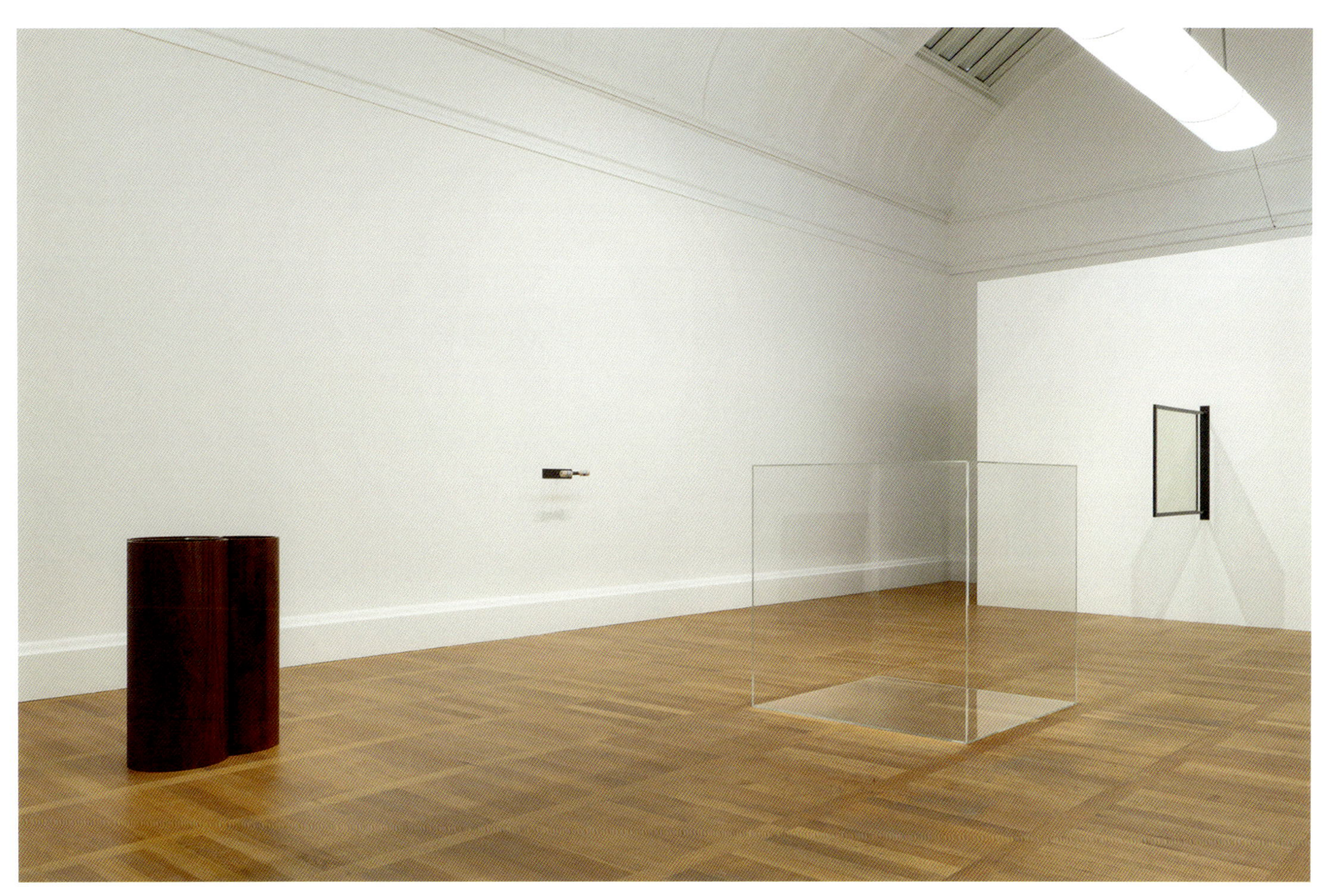

Epilogue   Daniella Rose King
This book came together alongside the exhibition *An Alterable Terrain*. In the exhibition, Rhea Dillon presents a series of works:
one existing, five newly created, that comprise fragments of an amorphous body. Occupying Gallery 30, the home of Art Now
at Tate Britain, Dillon approached the space as a container for the body. Viewed from below, its roof and rafters resemble
an overturned ship's hull. Simultaneously, the architecture conveys a human spine. These visual codes deeply enmesh those of the
slave ship, recalling histories tethered to geographies of the transatlantic and the experiences of transnational black diasporas.

95

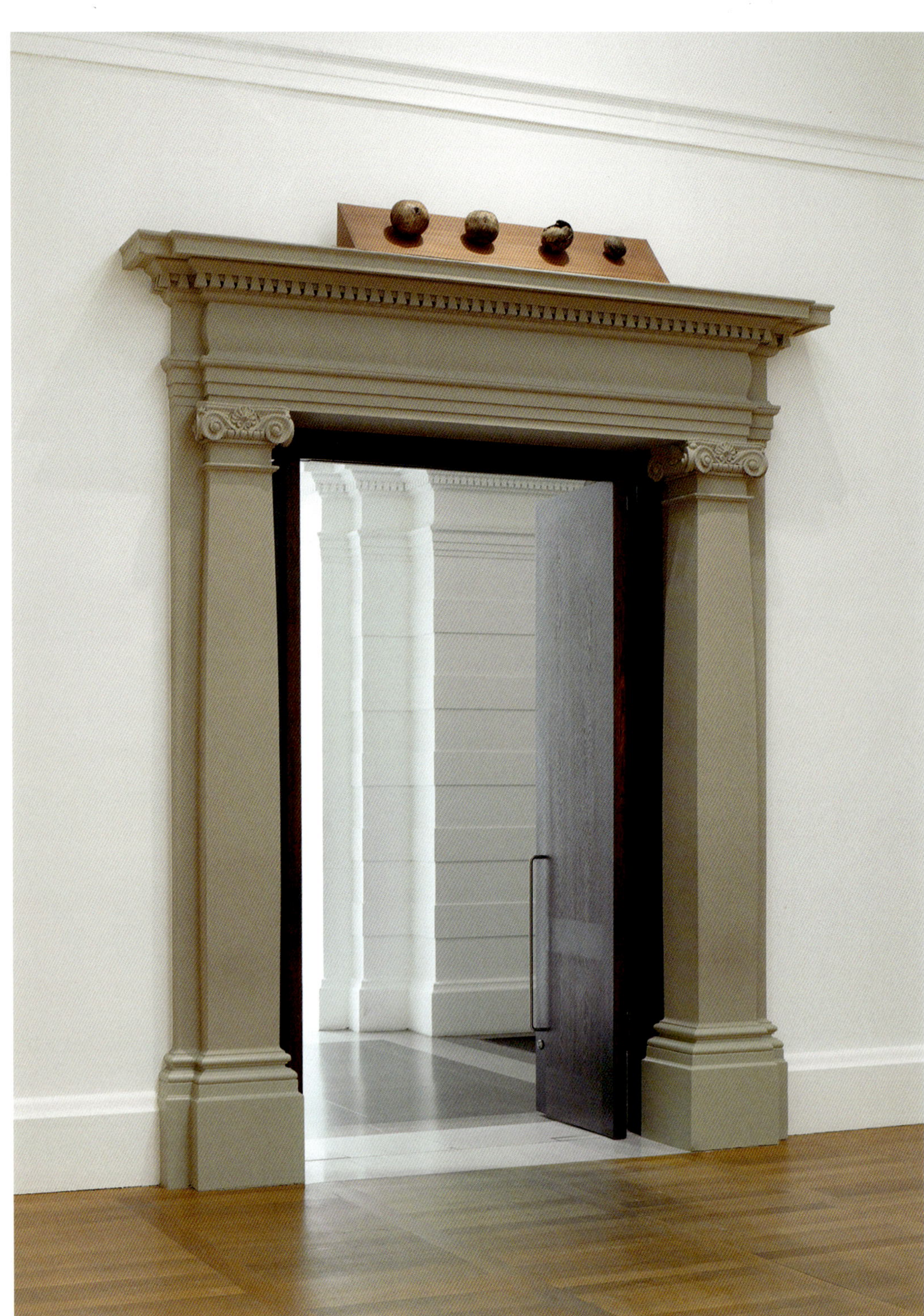

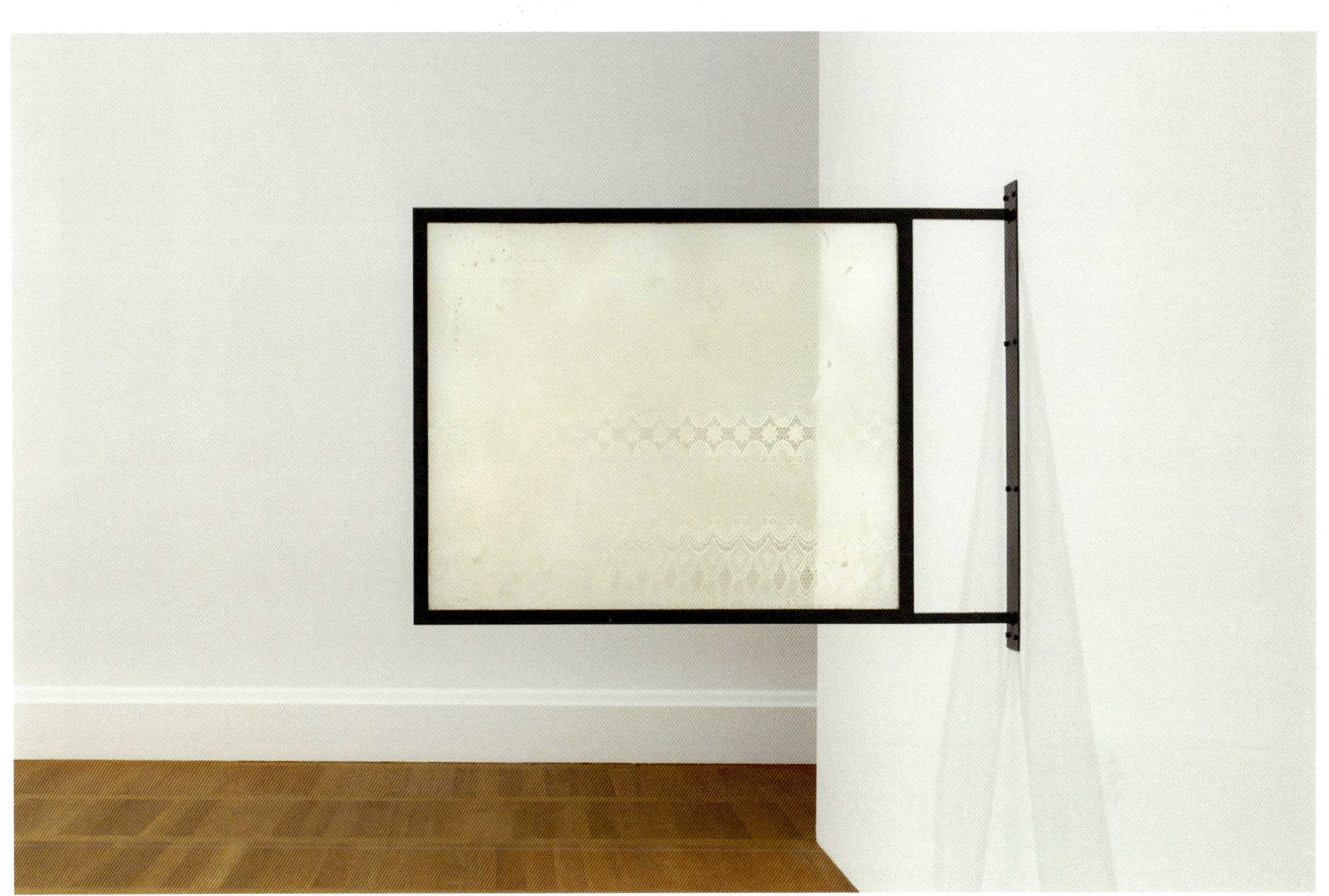

Eyes
The eyes are inferred by *Flagging Visions Of Periphery* 2023. A net curtain reminiscent of those at Dillon's grandmother's house is suspended in a pane of resin, surrounded by a steel frame that projects at a ninety-degree angle from the wall. Framing the act of seeing/looking, visitors' vision will be somewhat obscured in the manner that net curtains are used

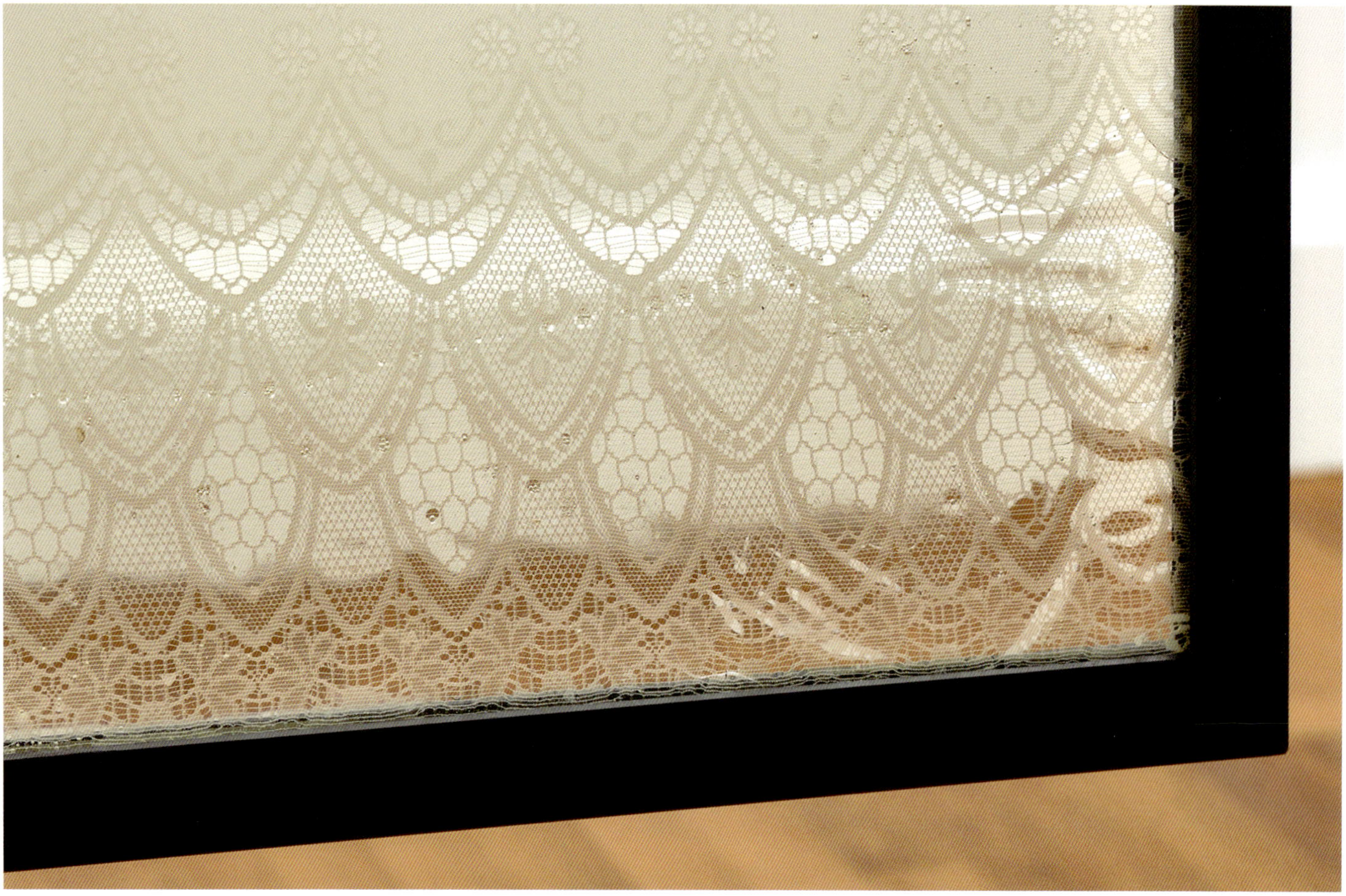

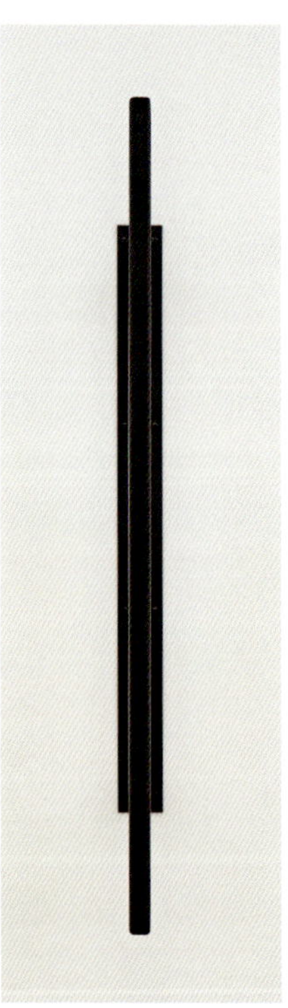

to allow light into a room but also provide privacy. This semi-translucent window further acts as a flag. This flag marks the terrain of the periphery, the marginalised geographies, the visible/invisibility of black women in the western imagination.

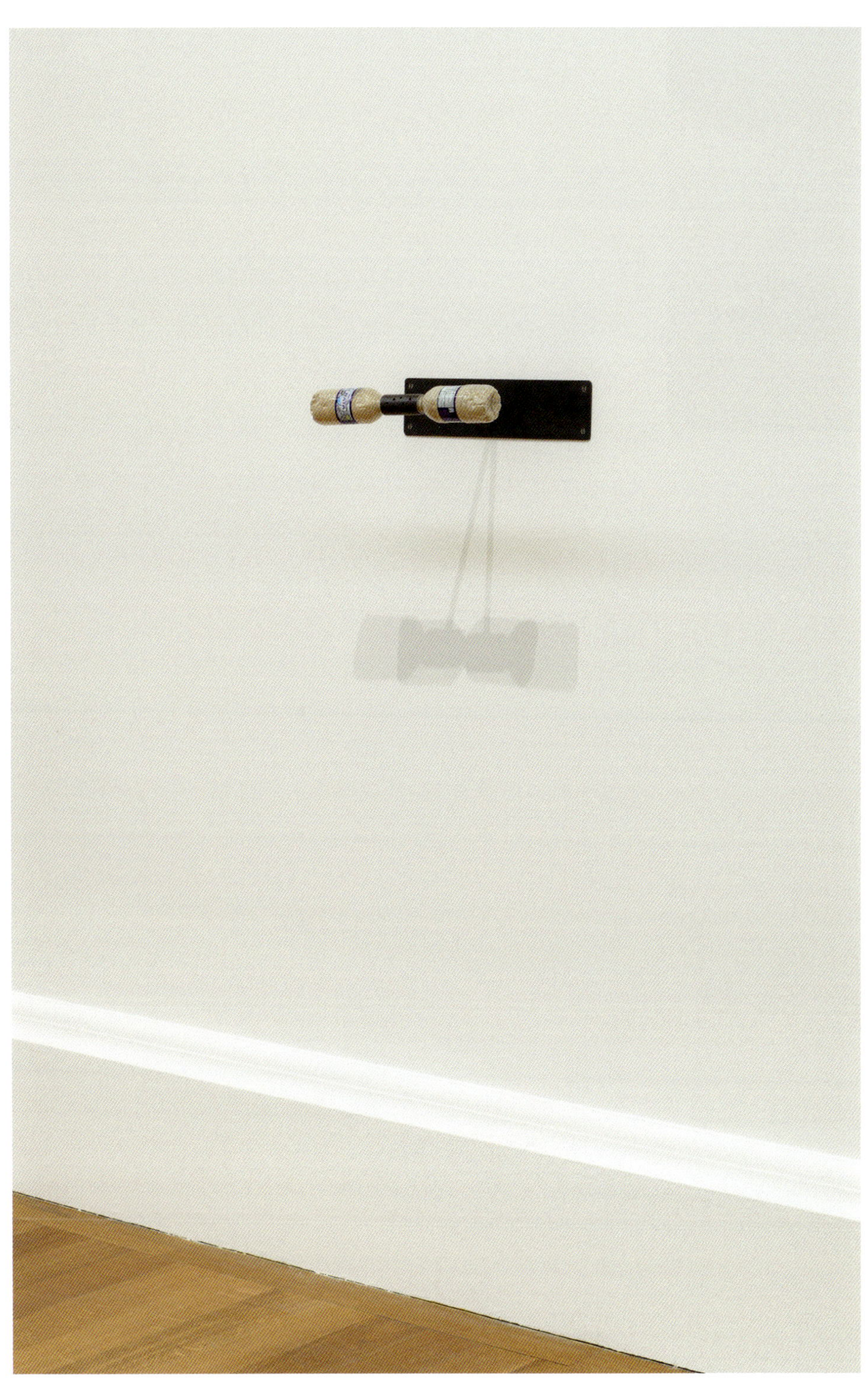

Mouth
As *Wata to Wine, Wine to Blood, Blood to Dirt, Dirt to Sand, Sand to Water; Wata (Bit)* 2023, in the artist's words, 'frames the chaos of black geographies and time by pausing it'[1] creating a sand timer held in a permanent state of horizontality and thus, limbo. The form is redolent of an iron bit used during the slave trade as a means of torture, preventing the subject

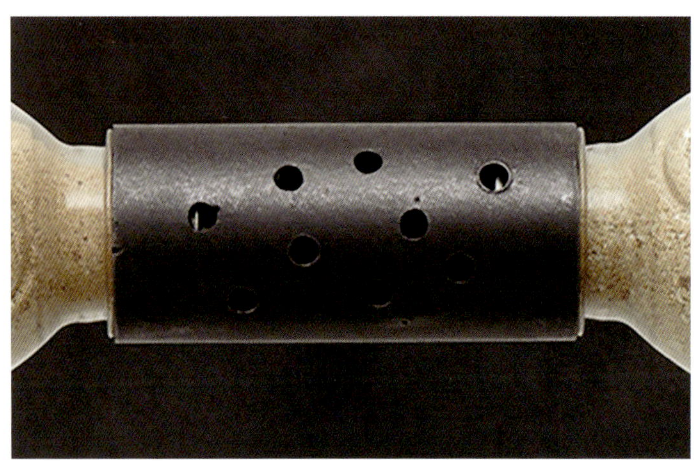

from speaking. Two plastic bottles (a Jamaican brand titled 'Wata') filled with sand from a beach in Trelawny Parish are held in place by the bit, the sand referencing geological time and a report of a stolen beach (an unsolved scandal involving truckloads of sand being removed illegally). The bottles are a nod to those left at Ghana's slave castles as offerings for the dead, wherein

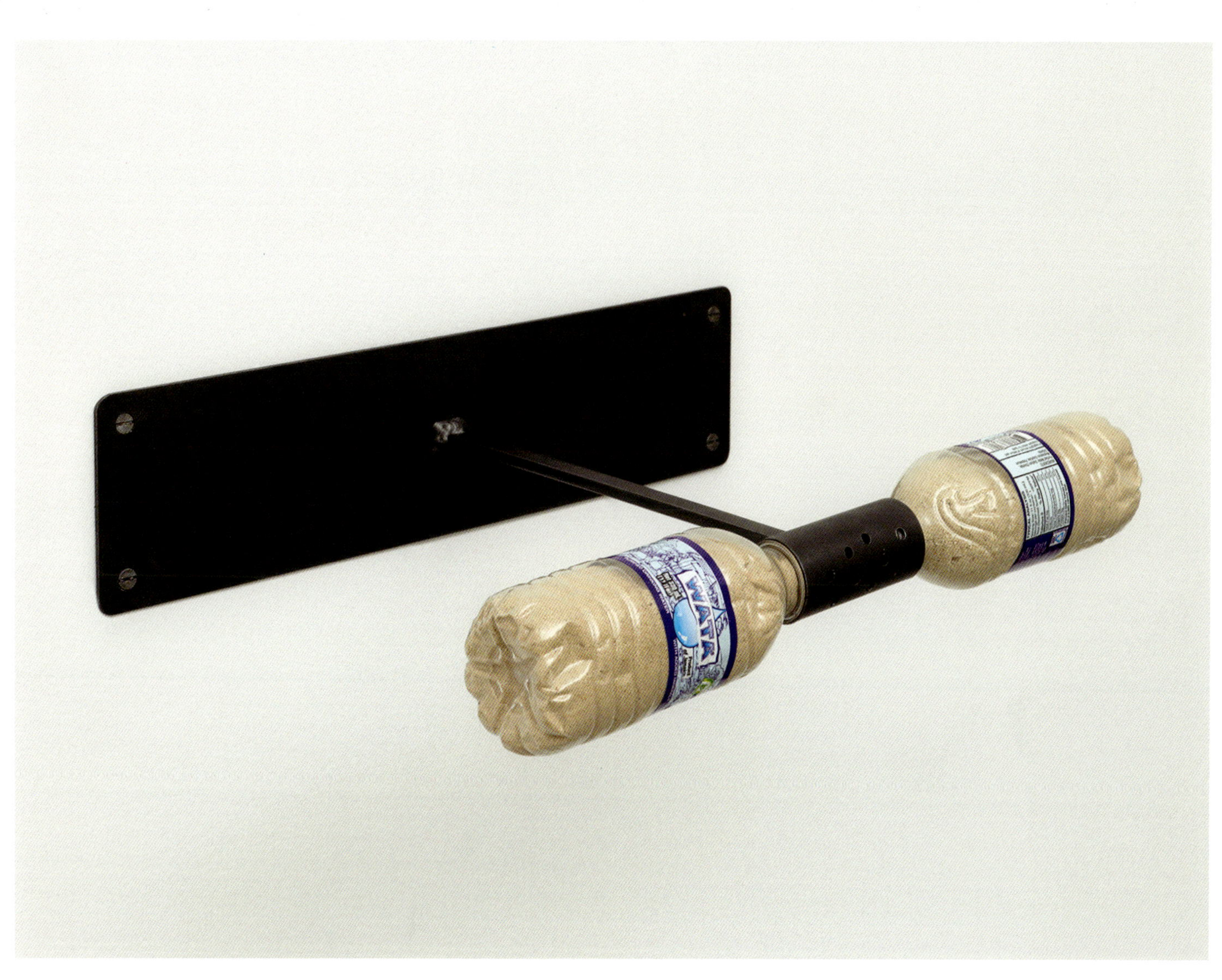

Dillon asks: 'what is a drink to the dry mouth of the dead?'[2] The stasis of the sand timer and this question highlights the ongoing erasures and terrors of the colonial project.

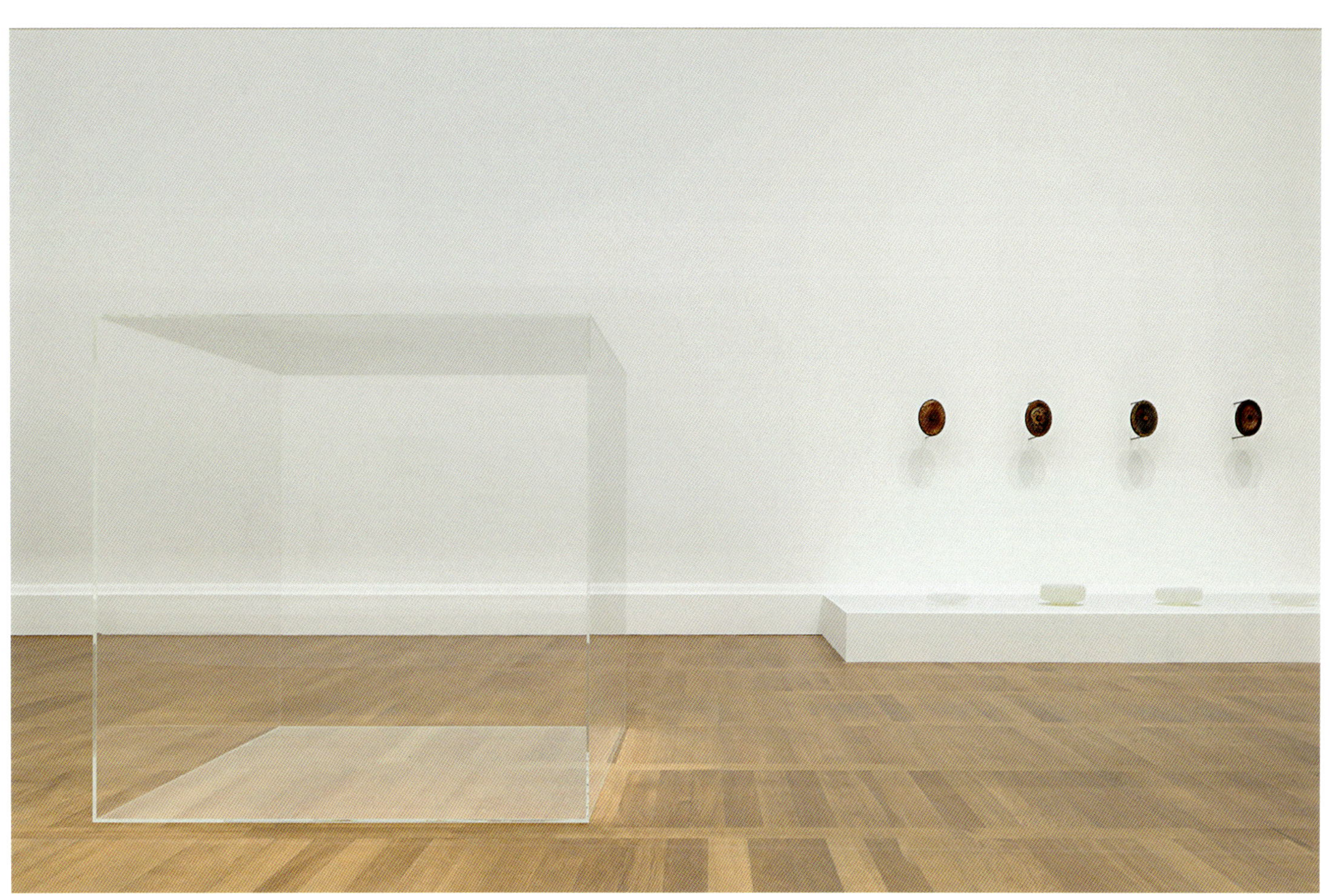

Lungs
In the centre of the gallery is a transparent cube titled, *Placing Her Within An Alterable Terrain* 2023. Measuring 160cm³, it is the average height of a woman today[3]. A fully enclosed space, the work acts as a tomb and touches on modes of containment and incarceration inherent to the site. Tate Britain is built on the site of the nineteenth-century Millbank penitentiary. How does its

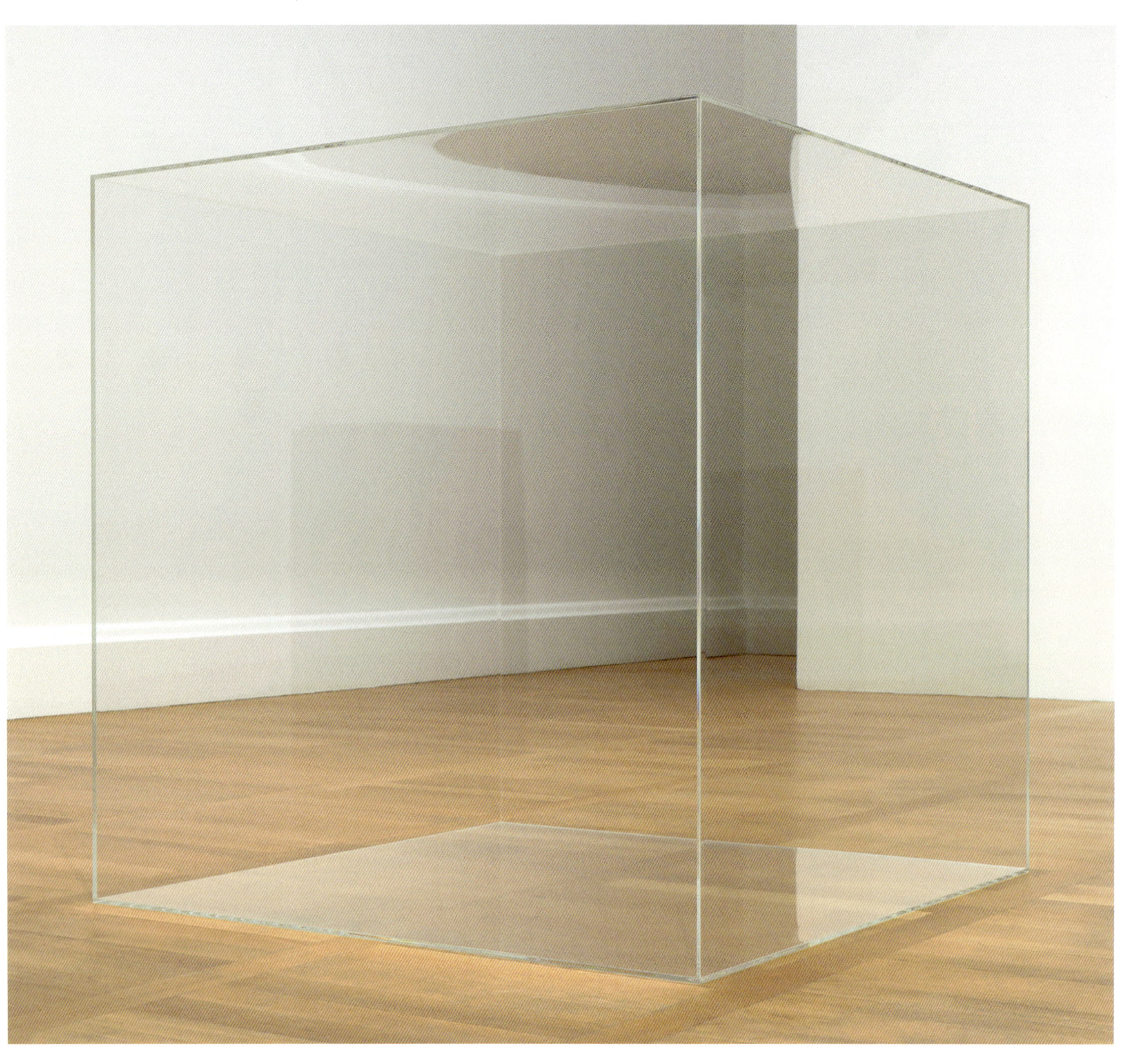

carceral historical landscape intertwine with that of the Caribbean colonial plantation and its violent afterlives? How do these physically distant geographies meet and come to bear on this space? How have the visual economies and ecologies of art and aesthetics upheld, reinforced and reproduced these landscapes and geographies? More urgently, perhaps, how can they unpick

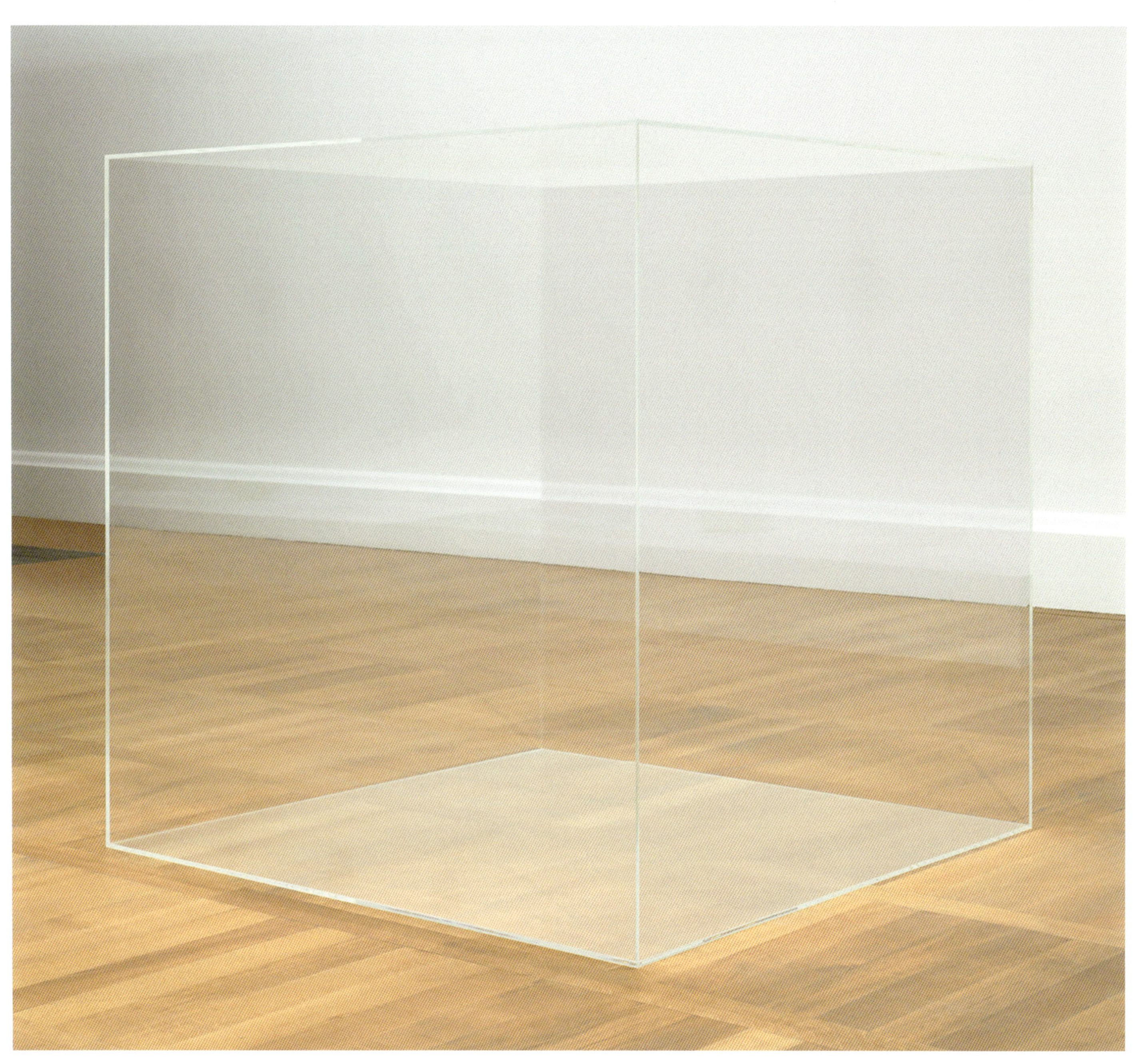

and unravel and deconstruct these terrains? Like bubbles of ancient air trapped in Antarctic ice, mined for information about the changing climate, the air within *Placing Her Within An Alterable Terrain* is a time-stamped portrait of the air we once breathed in London, in all its toxic and life-giving paradoxes. The lungs of this disembodied body allude to the air necessary for all of life,

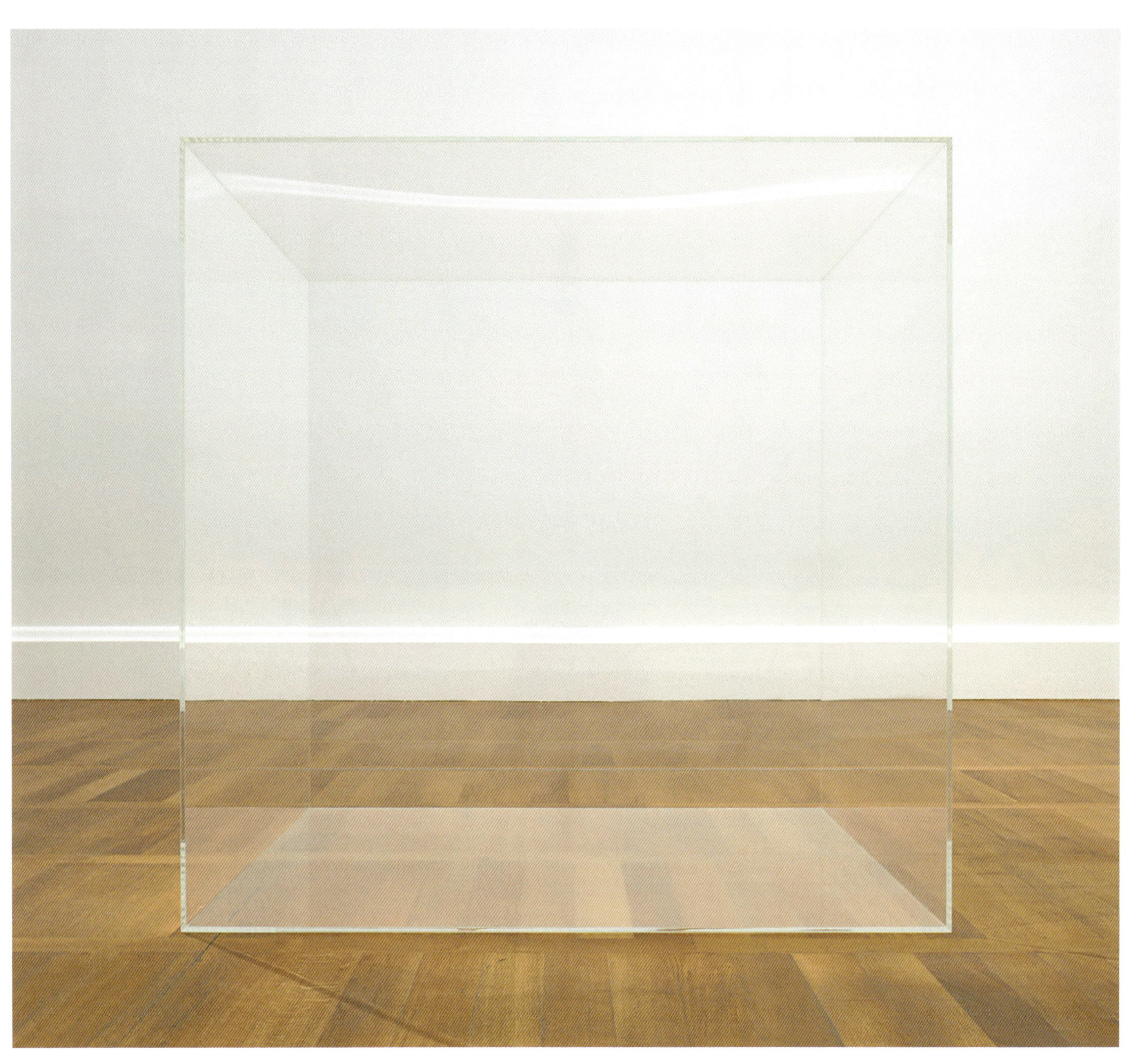

for respiration and speech. They suggest the deadly effects of air pollution due to environmental racism, and indisputable links between the climate crisis and the life of the transatlantic slave trade, what scholars have christened the Plantationocene and/or Racial Capitalocene. This box renders the breath lost and stolen from historical and future black subjects.

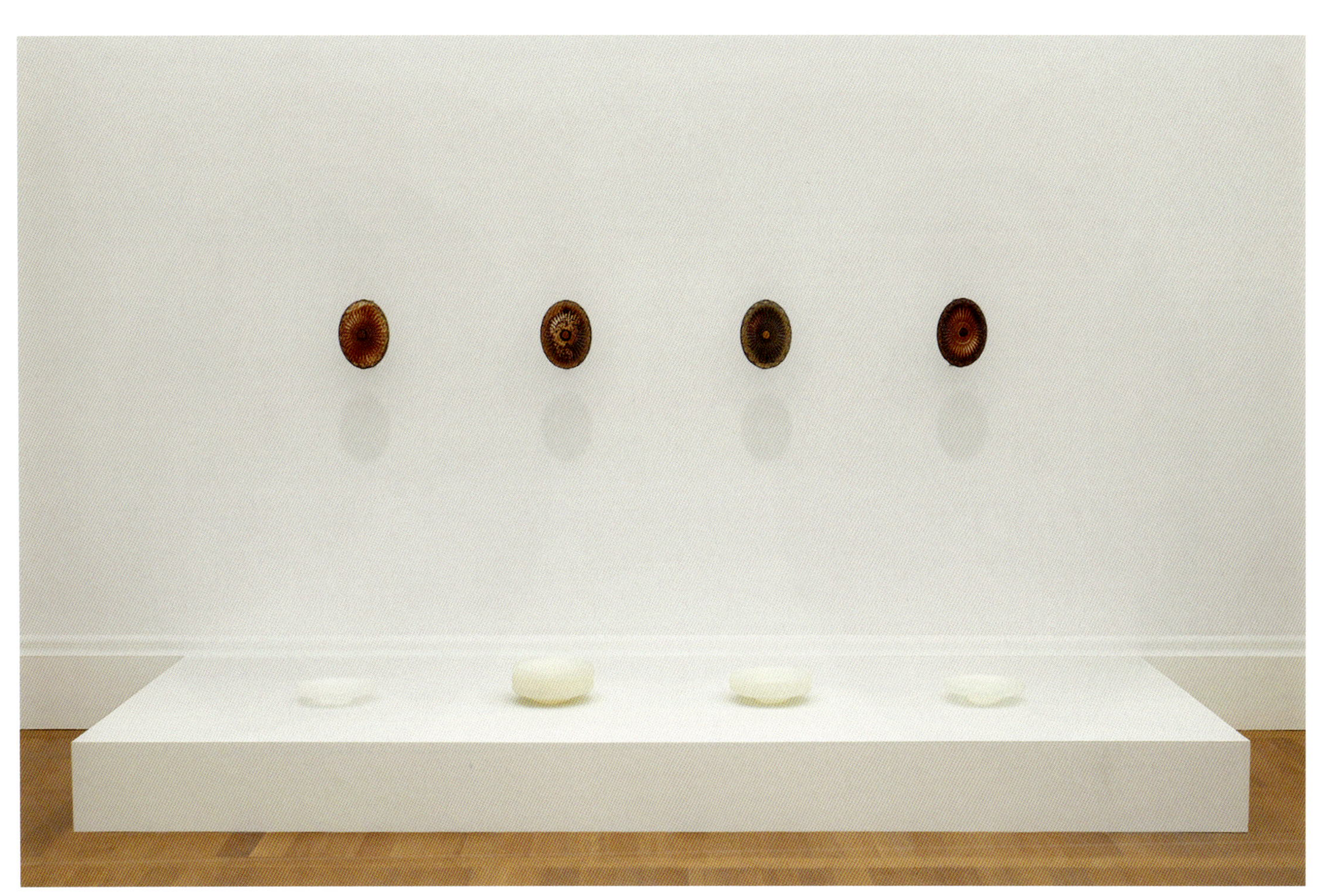

Hands & Feet
Displayed on both the wall and a low plinth are a series of objects that correspond with the hands and feet of this abstracted body.
The appendages that perform the labour of the body are manifest by Dillon as a number of plates titled *C/leaning Figures* 2023.
Made of cast resin mixed with molasses, and soap mixed with a scent of Dillon's own formulation, the plates speak to the

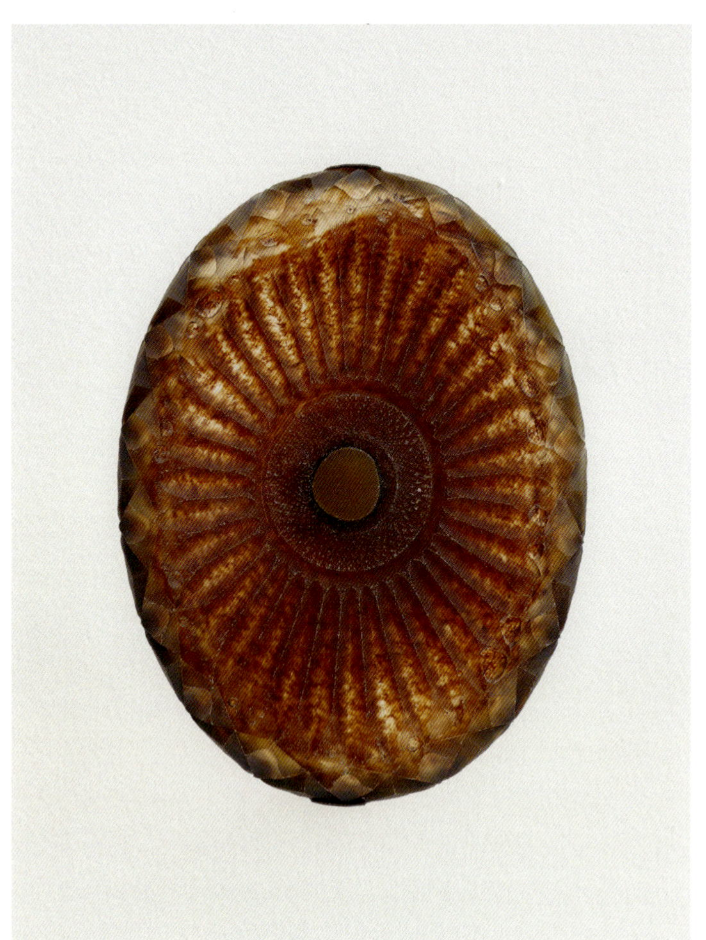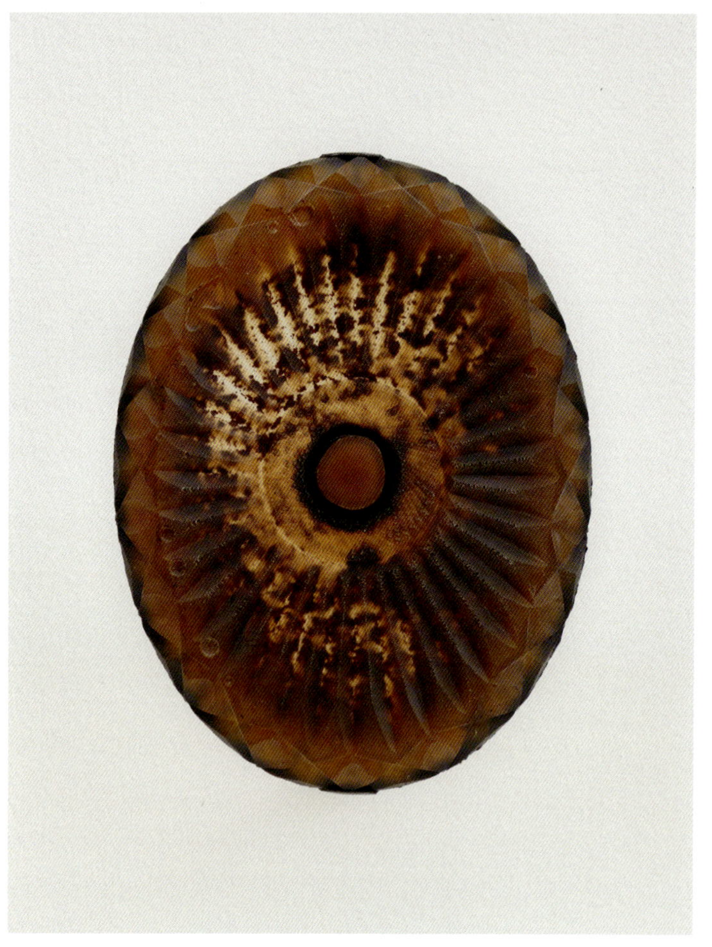

reproductive labour of domestic work and the aesthetics of the Caribbean diasporic home (one where a mahogany cabinet may contain a trove of these cut crystal objects for when 'the queen came [sic] to tea')[4]. The cast materials allude to specific aspects of labour from the Caribbean colonial plantation – the back-breaking labour of growing and cutting and processing sugar cane – to

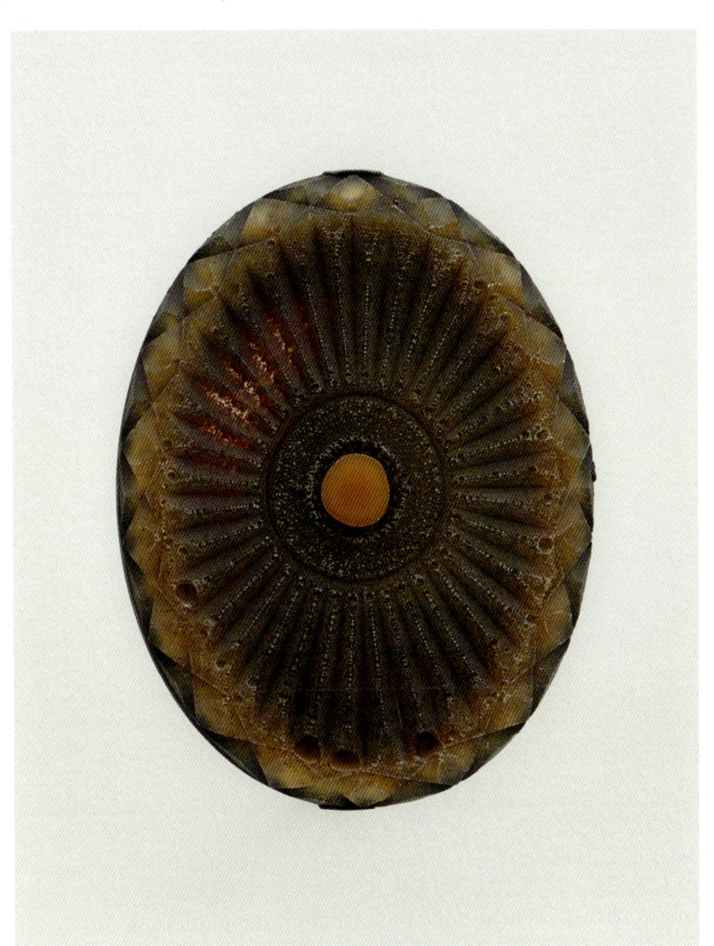 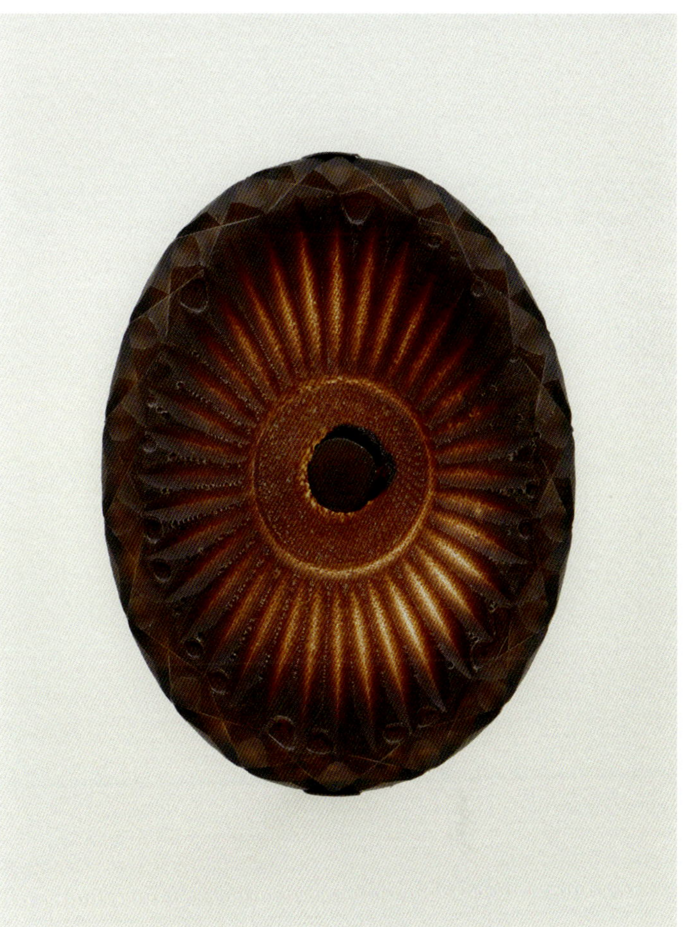

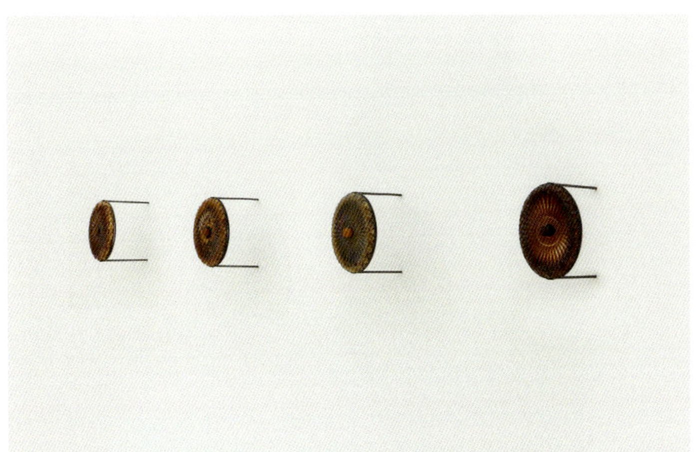

contemporaneous sites of largely outsourced, precarious, exhausting cleaning, domestic and care work in the UK. Dillon presents the darkest plates, those infused with the burnt sugar colour of molasses on the wall. They cast a warm glow onto the wall behind, and reveal the angles and patterns of the original crystal plates. Four stacks of pale, off-white plates are placed on a low plinth, almost in

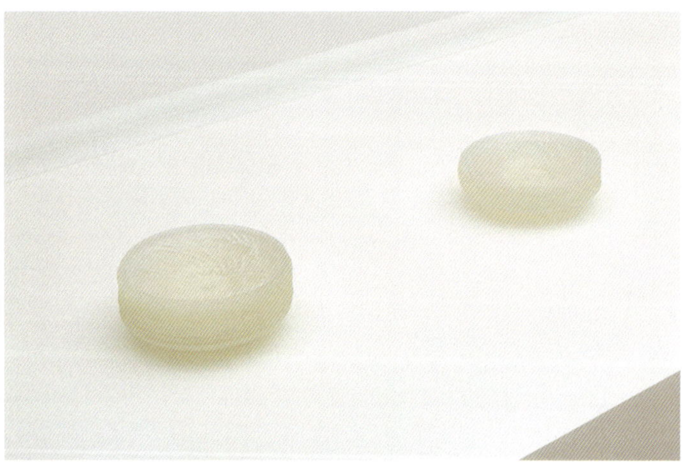

the brown plates' shadow, upending some visual/racial hierarchies. The stacks of plates encode the year of Jamaican independence – 1962 – into their formation, and offer a resting place for the labouring hands/feet. Dillon plays with the contradictions of the title, observing the exhausting body, leaning as it must, eventually against a wall, a plinth or any surface willing to support.

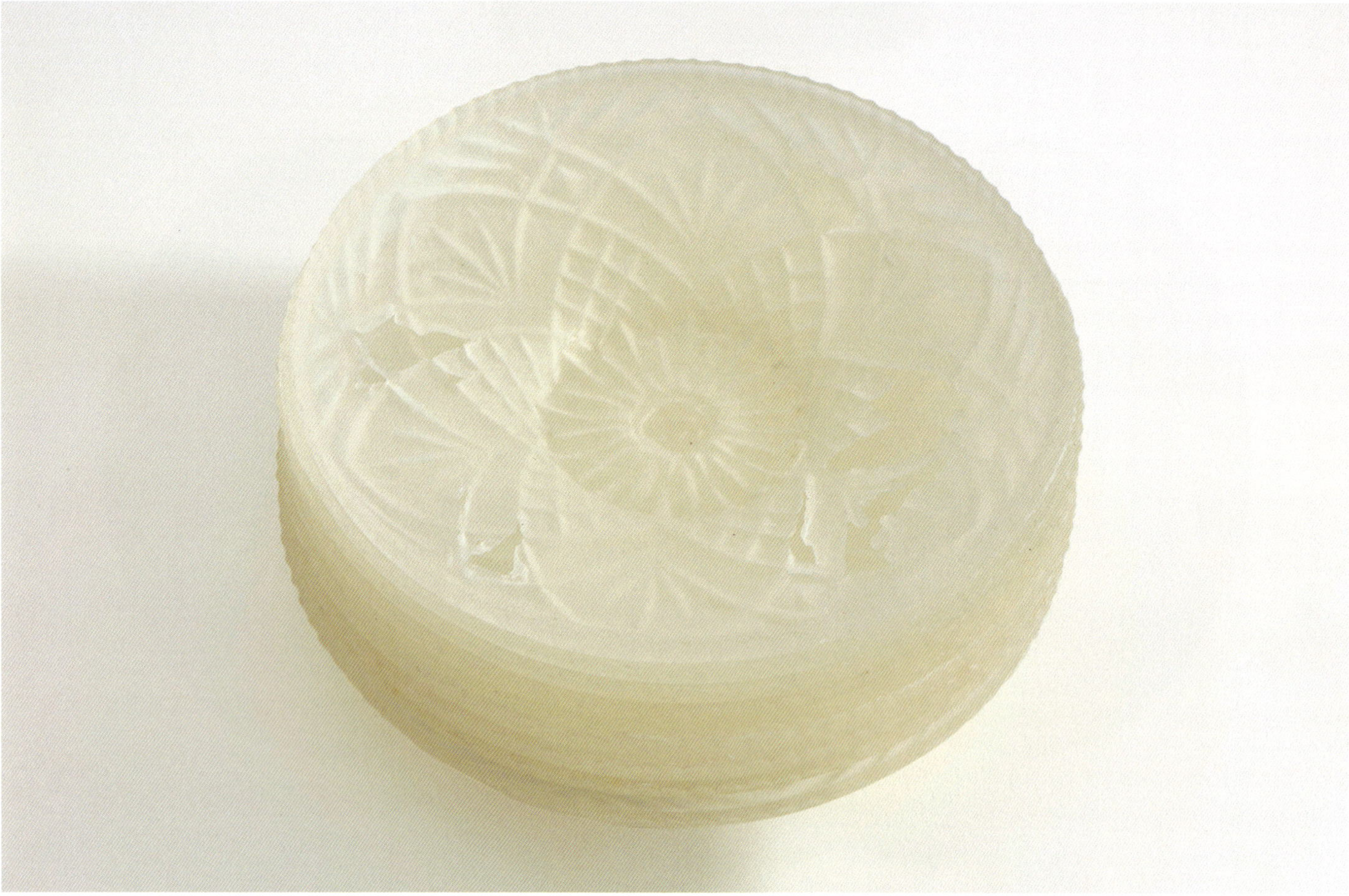

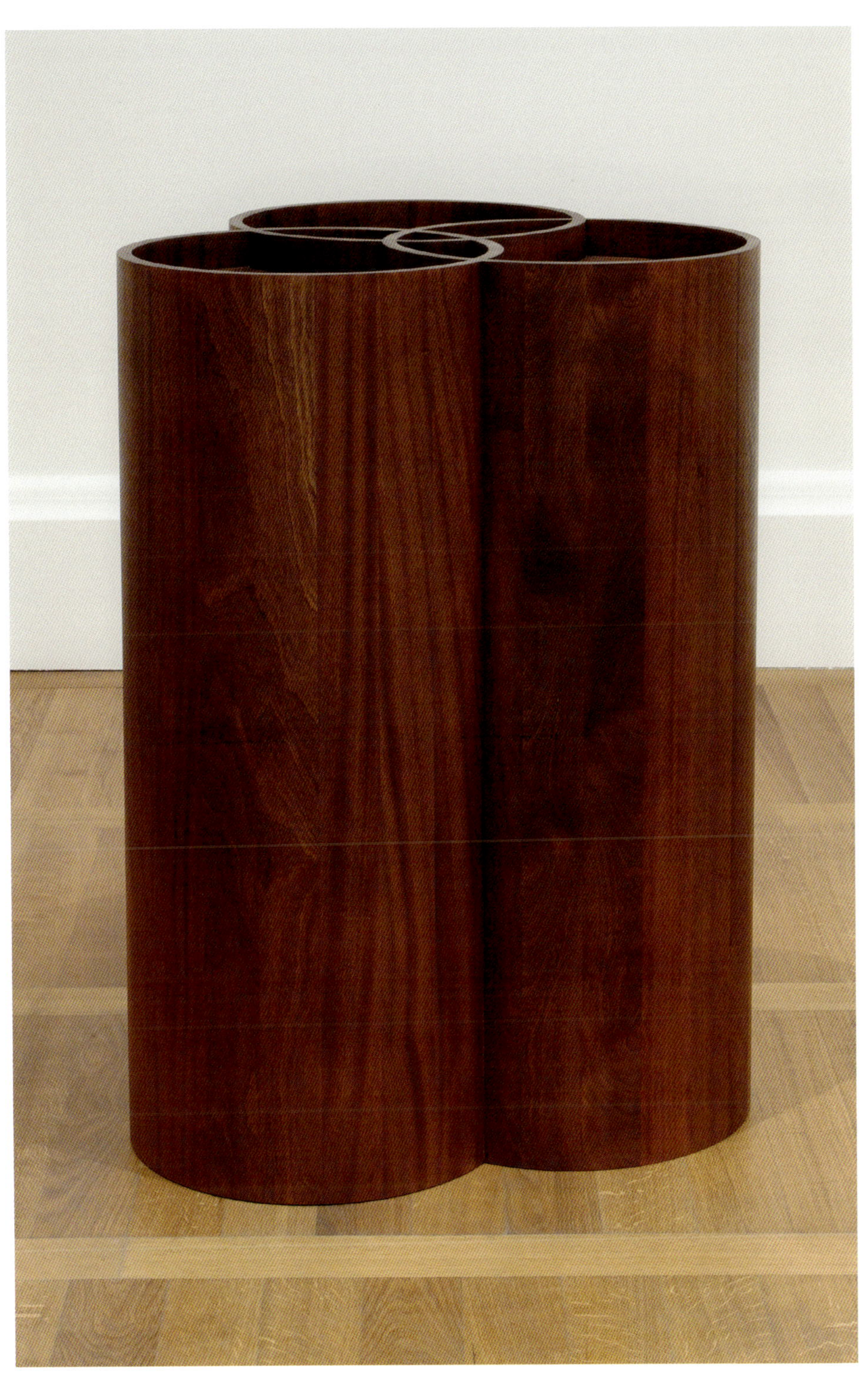

Soul
Entering the space of the gallery, the first work one encounters refers to the soul. Titled *An Unholy Trinity (the) Imaginary, Symbolic and Real* 2022 the mahogany sculpture is positioned on the floor, its height the same as a font in church. Its form recalls the plastic shipping barrels prominently used to transport souvenirs, dried foods, gifts, clothing, books and other objects between those in

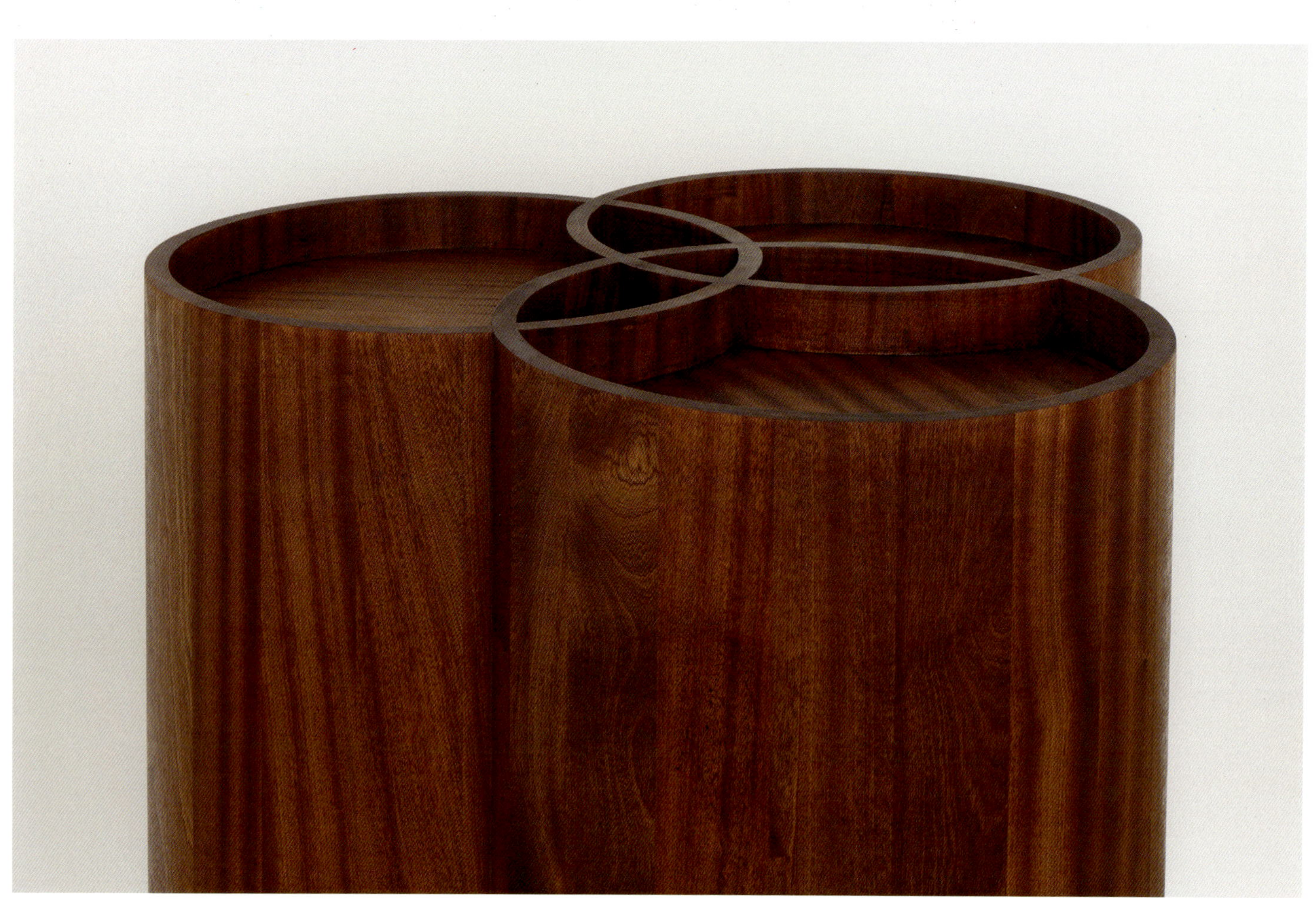

the diaspora, and between kin in the Caribbean. Viewed from above, one sees the interlinking loops are that of the Borromean knot; a mathematical symbol, not to mention a visualisation of the Holy Trinity in Christianity. The title is a direct reference to the psychoanalyst Jacques Lacan, who used the knot to describe three separate but intersecting spheres of psychic reality: the real,

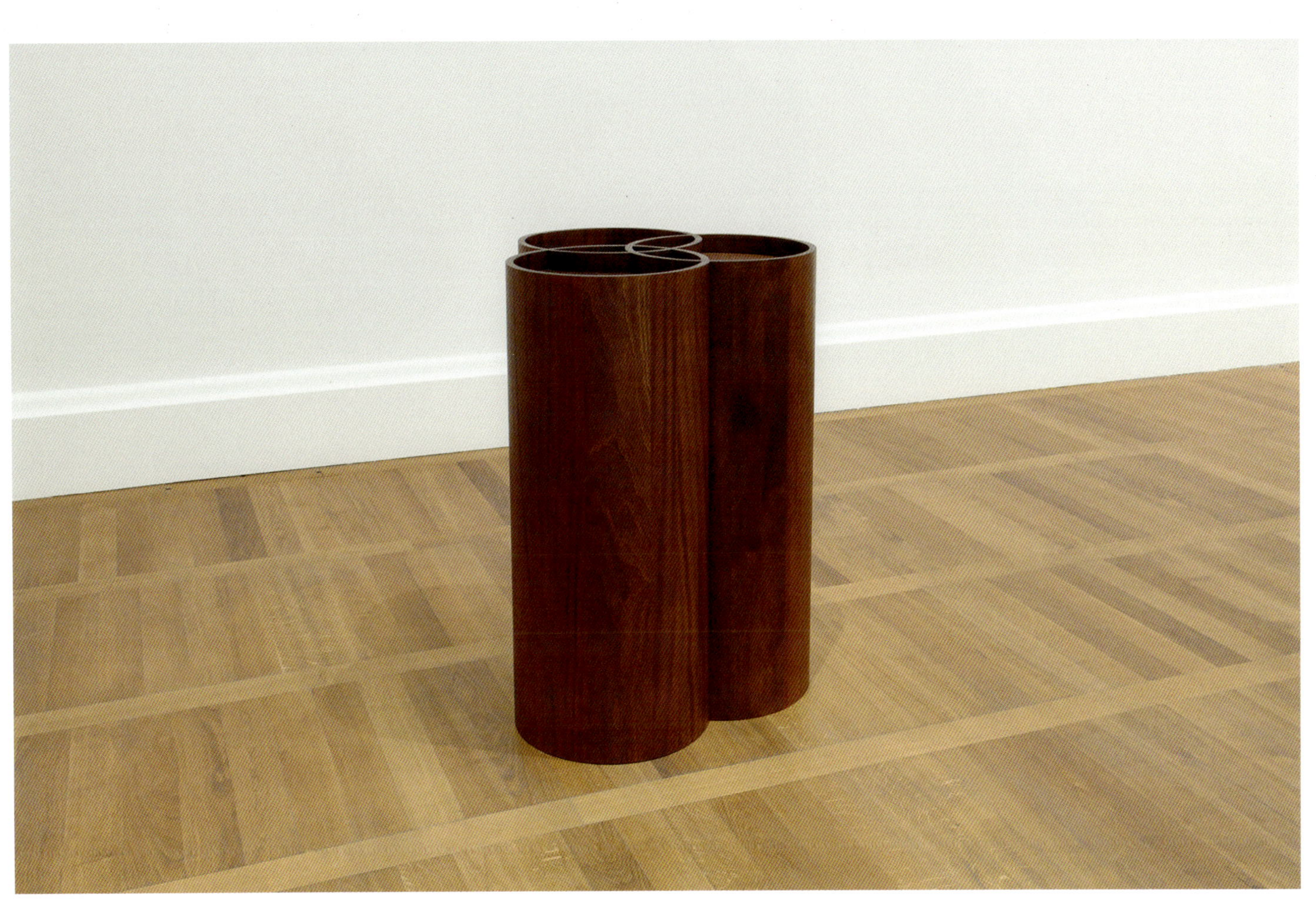

the symbolic and the imaginary. In the sculpture Dillon conjures Lacan's theorem to describe colonialism's presence in the makeup of Caribbean identities. The metaphor can be extended for the exhibition, where the fragmented (psychic) body can be viewed as a series of six interrelated and overlapping 'rims' (soul, hands and feet, eyes, mouth, reproductive organs, lungs).

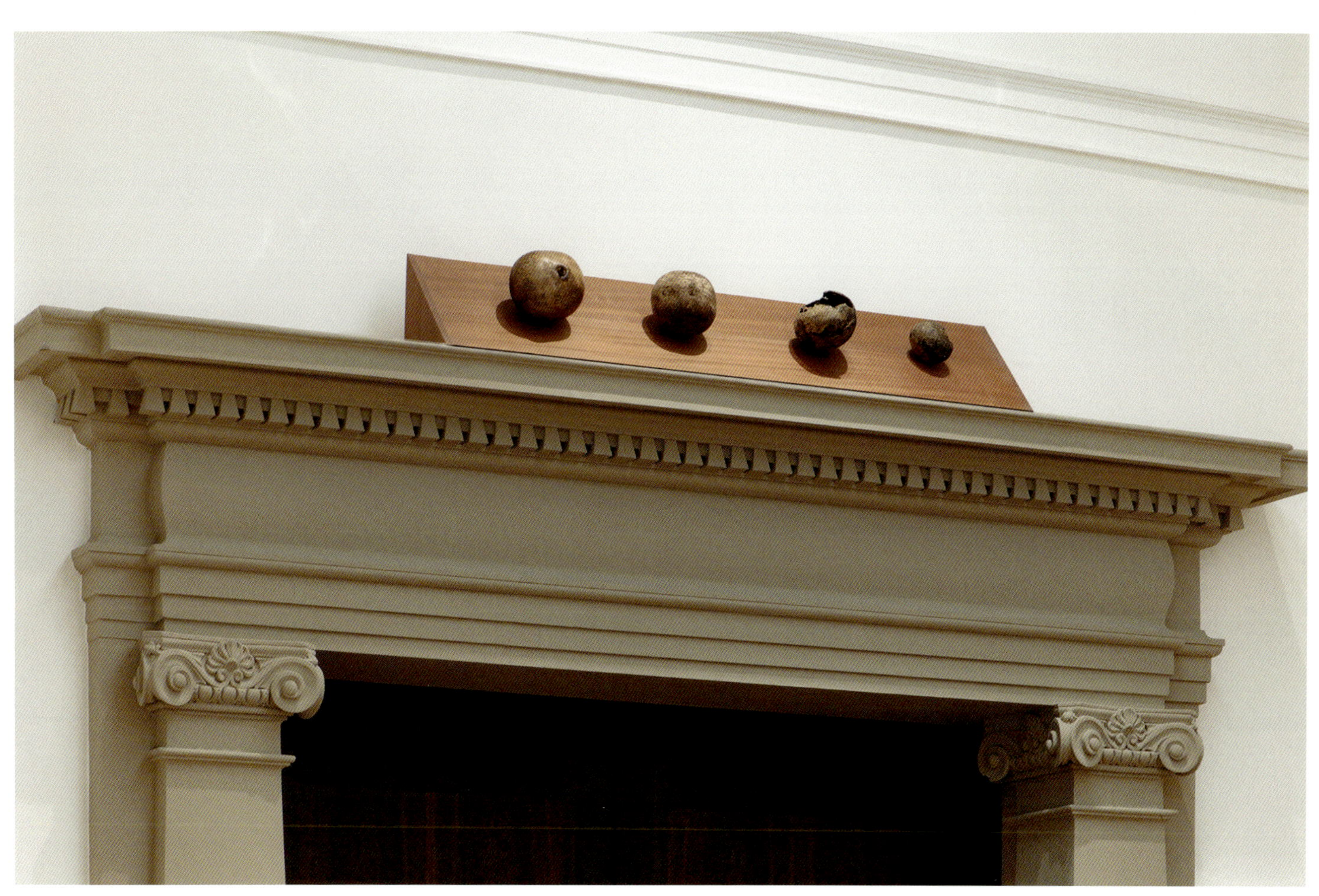

Womb, Breasts & Vagina
Positioned discreetly over the doorway is a work that is an abstraction of the female body's reproductive organs
(the womb-breasts-vagina). A mahogany ledge sits up high, above the entrance to the gallery, and has fixed upon it four
dried calabashes, collected from a farm in Maroon Town in Jamaica's Cockpit Country in January 2023. Presented as a

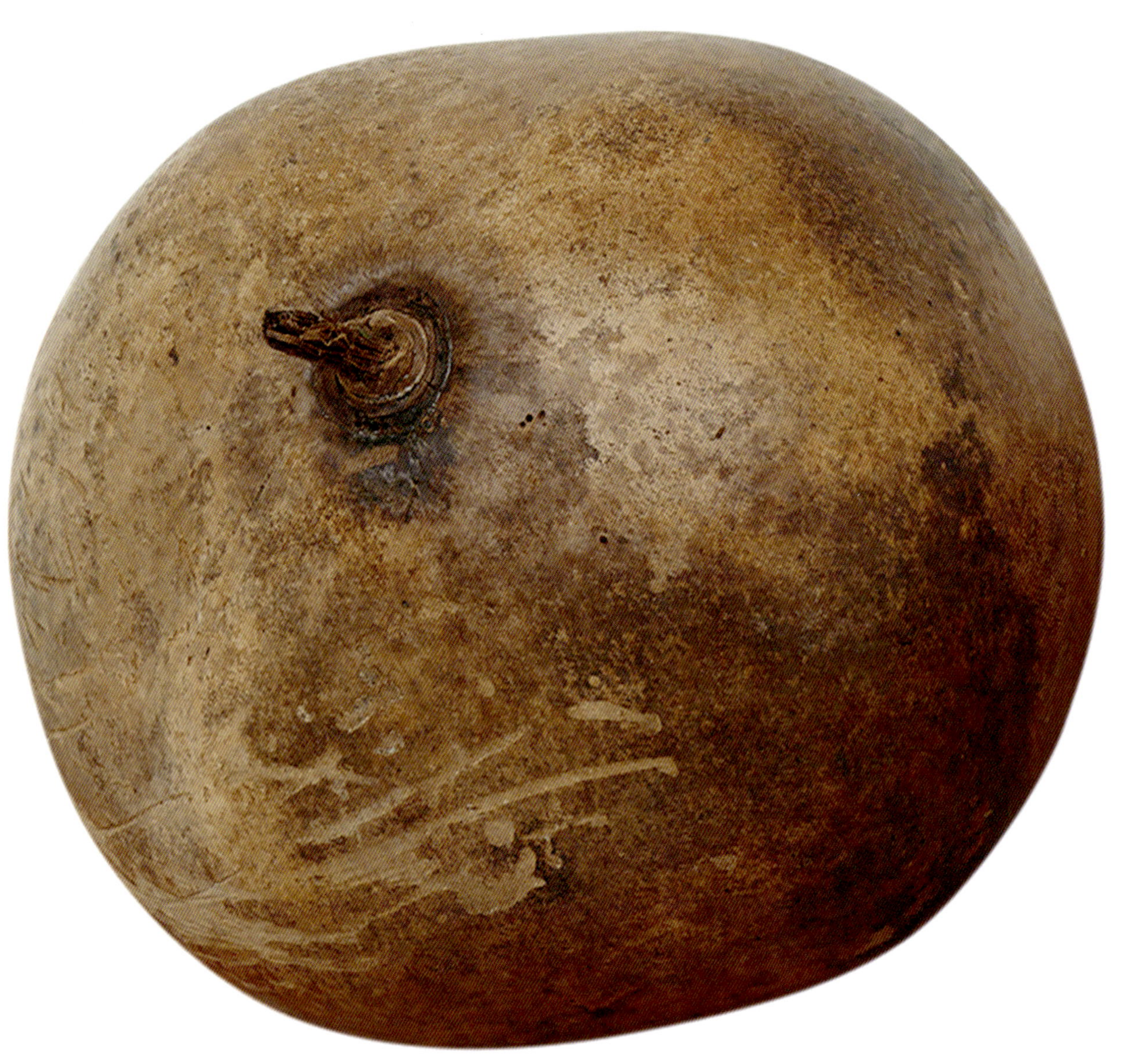

tableau and an altar, the work contends with the intimate terrorism beset upon black women's bodies, as the fulcrum of the slave trade, as machine of reproduction. The tableau suggests a 'discordant'[5] range of conditions – from whole to broken – where the womb/woman (said quickly the words sound the same) is represented ambivalently by the calabash and positioned as

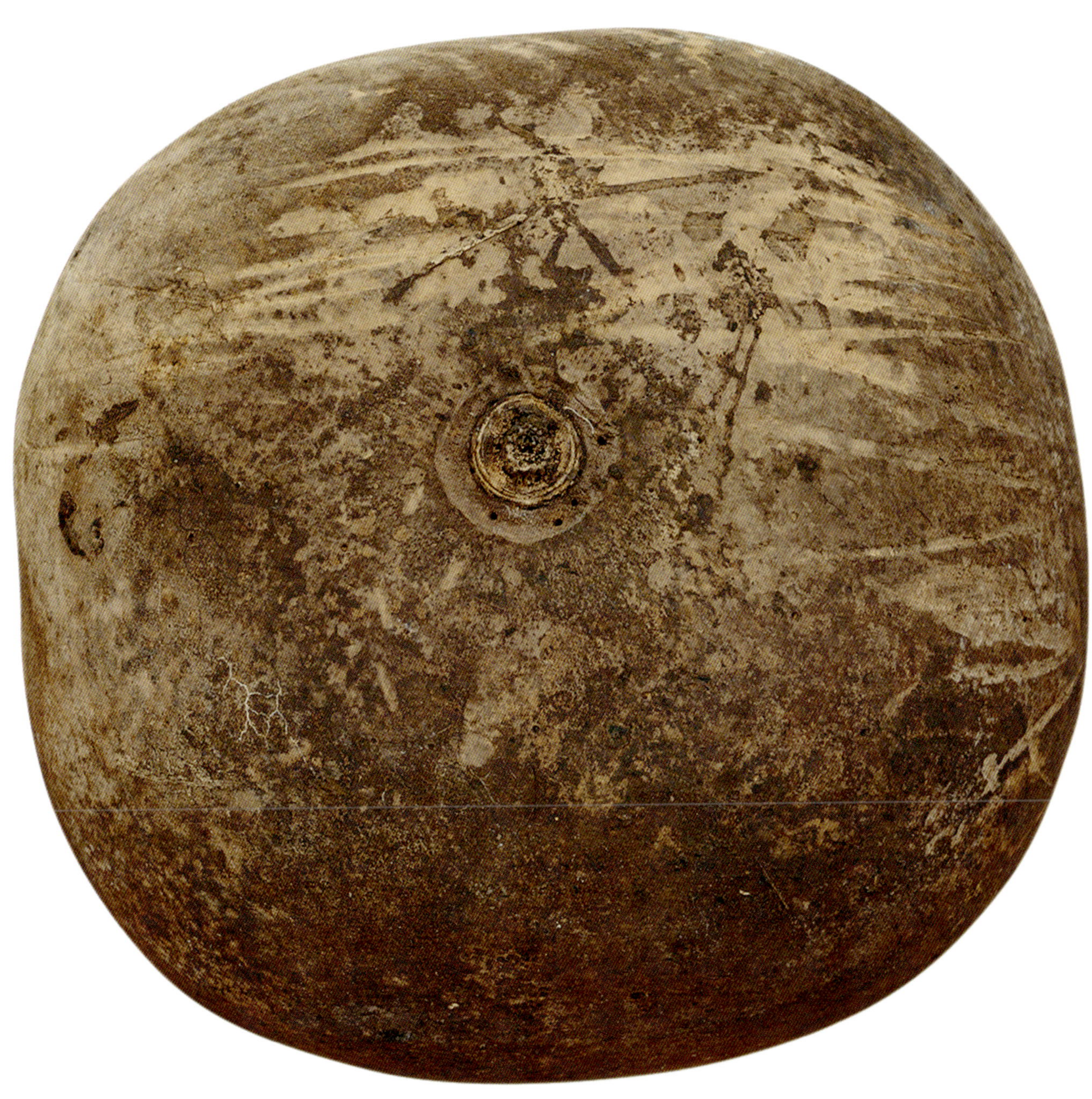

vessel, a 'public object'[6] and a ruin. This sculpture's title takes the form of a poem: *Swollen, Whole, Broken, Birthed in the Broken; Broken Birthed, Broken, Deficient, Whole–At the Black Womb's Altar, At the Black Woman's Tale* 2023. The title and the sculpture move us back and forth through these interchanging conditions: birth and sickness/death,

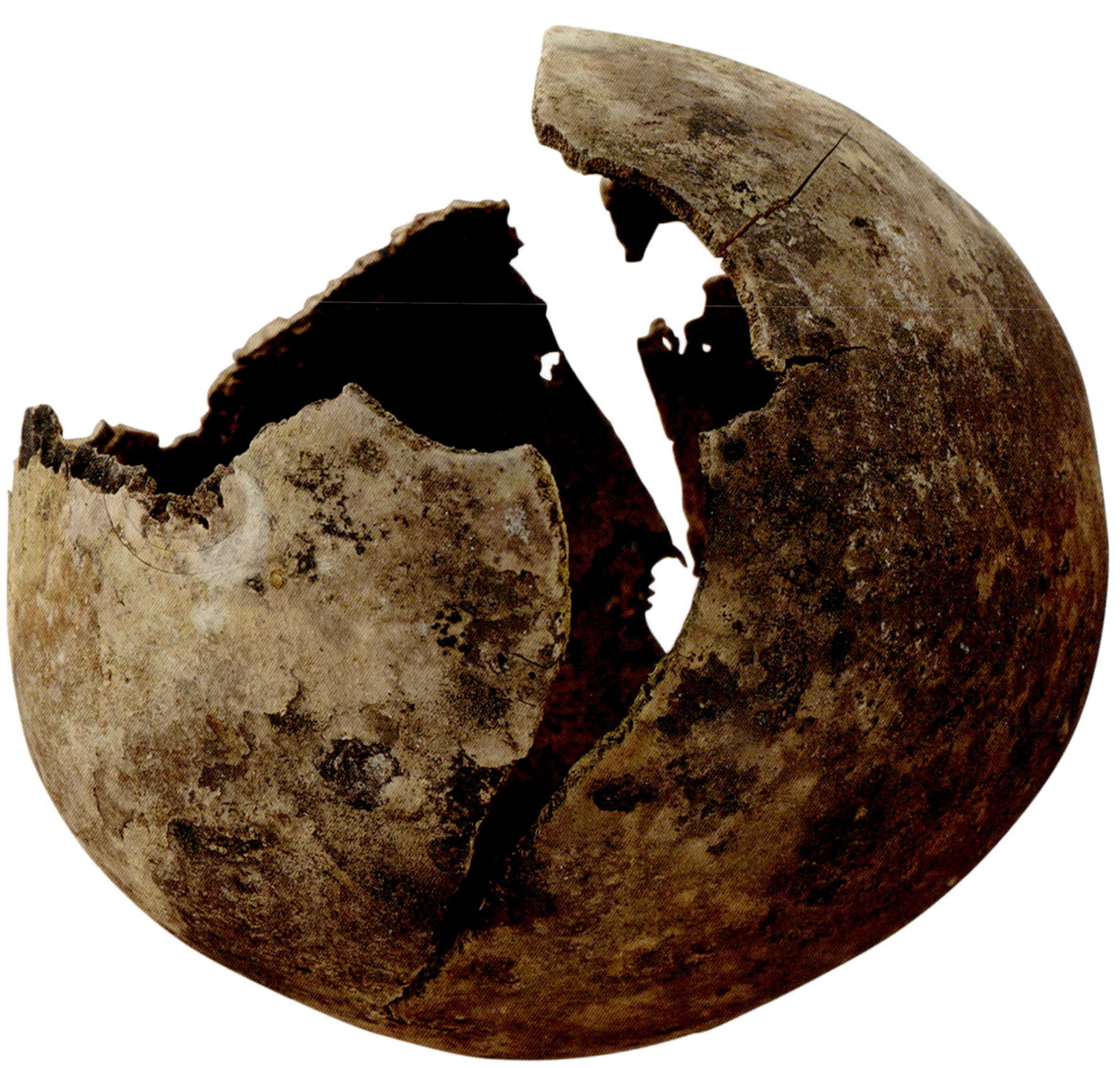

pleasure, extraction and worship; holding together these discordances as another mode of amorphicity. *An Alterable Terrain* maps a range of materials, referents, eras, spatial relations and epistemes onto the geography of the exhibition. Calabashes from the mountainous region of Maroon Town, the sands of a 'stolen' beach in Trelawny Parish, mahogany

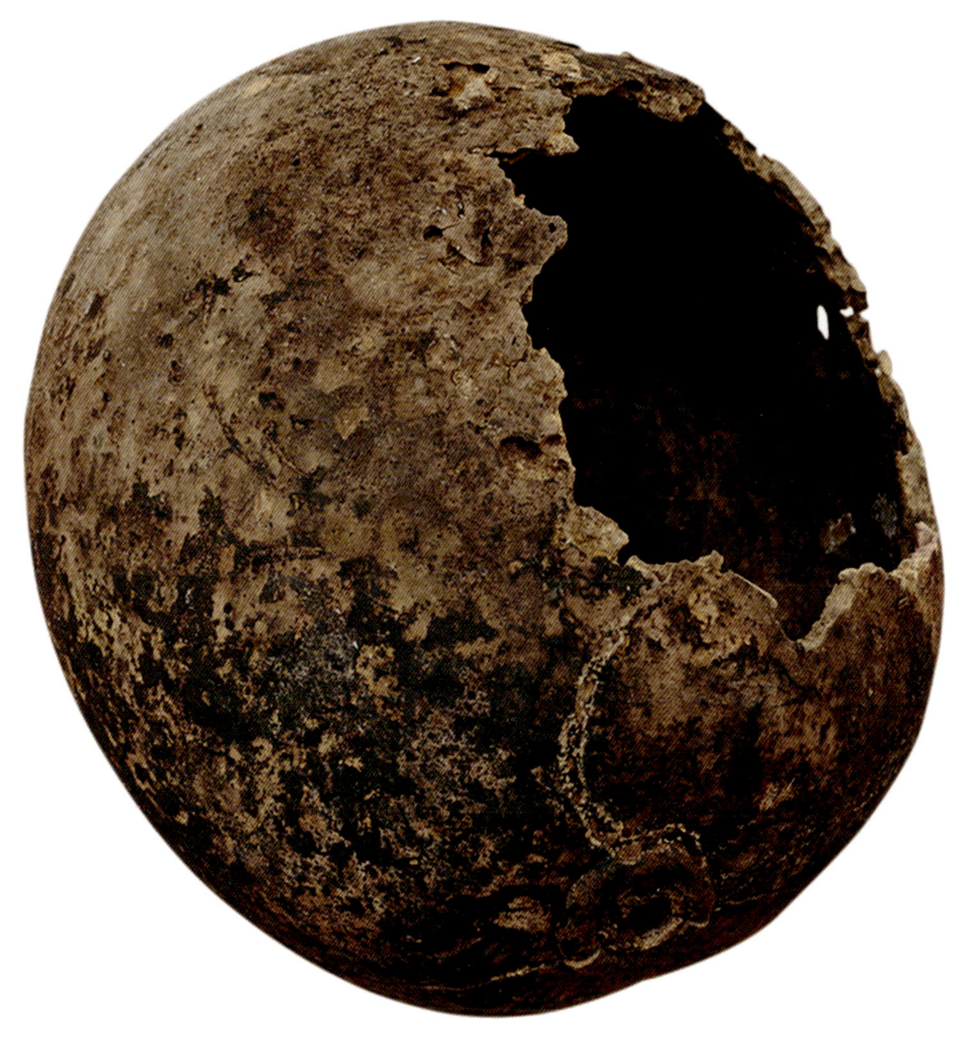

from West Africa, iron from the deep earth, molasses from Jamaican sugar cane, net curtains from grandma's living room – all collide with questions of geological time, plantation time, the time of the working day, non-linear non-western time, CP time, the frozen time of grief and death and the spirit. These fragments, tied as they are to memories, theories

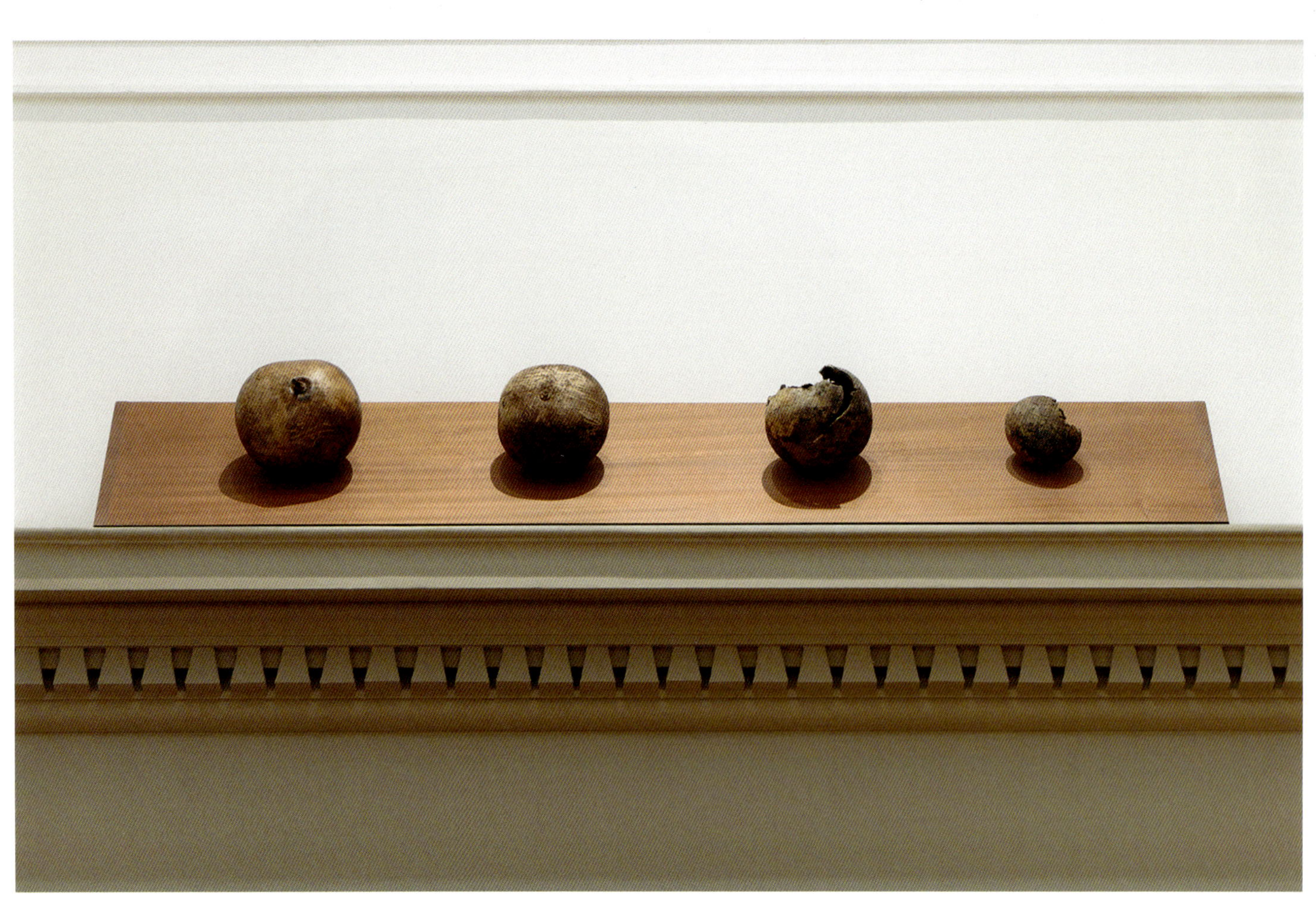

and writings connected to psycho-geographies of the transatlantic slave trade and practices of extraction and terror, call upon the very fact of black women's aliveness, waywardness, tricksterism, survival, amorphicity and the possibility of an alterable terrain.

The gallery is set (elevated) mere meters from the River Thames, a waterbody steeped in histories of the transatlantic slave trade. It is a liquid register of the memories of those trafficked and their extracted human labour, the very undergirding of the capital that flooded the city and country. As time has passed (400 years), laws have changed (emancipation), the market has evolved (plantation to neoliberal capitalism) and flows of capital have filtered through public and private life. Yet, the literally and valuably invisible[7] physical, intellectual, social, affective and reproductive labour of scores of black women and women of colour continues to underpin and sustain society. The fragments of the body contained within *An Alterable Terrain* are that of a black woman, displaced by historical forces from the African continent to the Caribbean archipelago and latterly to Western Europe. Historical forces of capitalism, colonialism and neoliberalism have prompted these movements; what Dillon calls 'landings' and 'arrivals', they are a litany of forced and chosen migrations, with elements of each in the other. Amorphicity is the desire here, where the subject's nebulous, fluid nature defies the logic of white supremacy, misogyny and racism. To be amorphous is to be mundane and complex, brilliant and quotidian, everything and nothing; resolutely human.

Summoning and probing material histories, aesthetic and political questions of minimalism and abstraction, historical representations and black feminist epistemologies, Dillon's works evoke fragments – including the eyes, hands and feet, mouth, soul, reproductive organs, and the lungs – of a conceptual figure. Viewed together, these disparate elements underline the foundational role black women's physical, reproductive and intellectual labour has played in the history of the British Empire. These pieces highlight links between historical sites of dispossession and contemporaneous sites of exploitation and overwork, arguing that these are ongoing, unending processes and forces. This assemblage of sculptures trouble how structures of power – including colonialism, racial capitalism and patriarchy – have an enduring presence in the production of Caribbean and British identities and lived realities. At the same time, and in the face of these structural lineages, the artist's objective is amorphousness.

Footnotes

1 Rhea Dillon, artist's unpublished exhibition notes,
  January 2023.
2 Ibid.
3 The artist calculated an average height from measurements
  collated from numerous websites including: Medical News
  Today and Medicine Net. https://www.medicinenet.com/
  height_women/article.htm
4 *To Hold Truth on Your Tongue or in Your Hand:
  An Interview with Rhea Dillon* by Dara Jochum.
  (https://www.spikeartmagazine.com/?q=articles/hold-
  truth-your-tongue-or-your-hand-interview-rhea-dillon),
  last accessed 4 May 2023.
5 See this volume, Katherine McKittrick, 'Integers and Agony
  and Discordance'.
6 Katherine McKittrick, *Demonic Grounds: Black Women
  and the Cartographies of Struggle,* Minneapolis 2006, p.46.
7 Françoise Vergès, 'Capitalocene, Waste, Race, and Gender',
  e-flux, no.100, May 2019 (https://www.e-flux.com journal/100/
  269165/capitalocene-waste-race-and-gender/), last accessed
  4 May 2023.

Patricia Noxolo's Annotated Bibliography

CARICUK YouTube channel, 2021–2, https://www.youtube.com/channel/UCpVvZEqrk hdlK21SkWvkNmw, last accessed 31 March 2023. This YouTube channel was created by Pat Noxolo and a team of Black artists, academics and activists, in an Arts and Humanities Research Council-funded project (Creative Approaches to Race and In/security in the Caribbean and the UK). It contains films and discussion events around in/security, race, gender and climate change.

Idza Luhumyo, *Five Years Next Sunday* 2020, http://www.caineprize.com/the-stories-2022, last accessed 31 March 2023. This speculative short story, winner of the 2022 Caine Prize for African Writing, resonates beautifully with Rhea Dillon's exhibition. It is about a Kenyan woman who is a 'caller' – cutting her hair calls the rain. It has not rained for five years, and her hair is attracting a lot of attention…

Katherine McKittrick, *Demonic Grounds: Black Women and the Cartographies of Struggle,* Minneapolis 2006.
    This now classic book opened up the field of Black Feminist Geographies. It discusses Black women's spatial agency, during enslavement and into our environmentally-challenged futures.

Tiffany Onyejiaka, *Black Maternal Mortality is Already a Crisis – Climate Change is Making it Worse,* 2020 in Glamour, https://www. glamour.com/story/black-maternal-mortality-is-already-a-crisis-climate-change-is-making-it-worse, last accessed 8 August 2023.
    This article interviews the writer of an influential US report on Black Maternal Mortality, identifying the ways in which climate breakdown is exacerbating poor outcomes for Black women in the US.

Françoise Vergès, *A Decolonial Feminism,* London 2020. This slim book reunites feminist thought with anti-capitalism and decolonisation. It presents powerful arguments for radical change.

Biographies

RHEA DILLON

Dillon is an artist, writer and poet based in London. Recent exhibitions include *We looked for eyes creased with concern, but saw only veils* at Sweetwater, Berlin (2023); *The Sombre Majesty (or, on being the pronounced dead)* at Soft Opening, London (2022); *Real Corporeal* at Gladstone Gallery, New York (2022); *Love* at Bold Tendencies, London (2022); an online screening at The Kitchen, New York (2022); Drawing a Blank curated by Ben Broome, London (2022); *Janus* at Soft Opening, London (2021) and *Uchronia et Uchromia* online at External Pages (2020). She was an artist in residence at Triangle - Astérides, Marseille and previously at V.O. Curations, London, which culminated in a solo exhibition, *Nonbody Nonthing No Thing* and the publishing of poetry chapbook, *Donald Dahmer* (both 2021). In 2021 Dillon presented *Catgut – The Opera* at the Serpentine Pavilion as part of Park Nights series and in 2023 she produced a publication of the same title with Worms Publishing.

PATRICIA NOXOLO

Professor Noxolo's research brings together the study of international culture and in/security, using postcolonial, discursive and literary approaches to explore the spatialities of a range of Caribbean and British cultural practices. Key publications include *Geographies of race and ethnicity 1: Black Geographies, in Progress in Human Geography* (2022), and *Dancehall In/securities: Perspectives on Caribbean Expressive Life* (2022). She was awarded the 2021 Royal Geographical Society (RGS) Murchison Award and is a Fellow of the Academy of Social Sciences. Noxolo has led two international teams exploring Caribbean in/ securities and creativity – CARISCC: Caribbean In/Securities: Creativity and Negotiation in the Caribbean and CARICUK: Creative Approaches to Race and In/security in the Caribbean and the UK, and is co-lead of University of Birmingham's Stuart Hall Archive Project. She also commissioned the report 'Supervising Black Geography PhD Researchers in the UK' (2021), and is co-founder of the Fi Wi Road internships for Black Geography of undergraduates. Noxolo is a committee member the RACE group of the RGS, former chair of the Society for Caribbean Studies, and former co-editor of Transactions of the Institute of British Geographers.

BARBARA FERLAND

Ferland was born in Spanish Town, Jamaica in 1919. She wrote the music for the first all-Jamaican pantomime, *Busha Bluebeard* (1949), lyrics by Louise "Miss Lou" Bennett-Coverley. She was a contributor to the BBC's *Caribbean Voices* in Jamaica in the 1950s and then settled in Britain in 1960. In 1994, *Without Shoes I Must Run* was published as a single anthology of Ferland's poetry and contains work from the *Caribbean Voices* period together with some previously unpublished poems written in Britain. She referred to her poems as 'jingles' as she preferred it that way.

ZOÉ SAMUDZI

Samudzi is the Charles E. Scheidt Visiting Assistant Professor of Genocide Studies and Genocide Prevention at the Strassler Center for Holocaust and Genocide Studies at Clark University, Massachusetts, as well as a Research Associate at the Center for the Study of Race, Gender, and Class at the University of Johannesburg. She is an associate editor with *Parapraxis Magazine*, and a writer and critic.

FRANÇOISE VERGÈS

Vergès is a decolonial feminist theorist, an antiracist and anti-imperialist activist and an independent curator. She writes on systems of domination, the afterlives of slavery and colonialism, the decolonial 'post-museum', racial capitalism and practices and theories of struggles and resistance.

VANESSA ONWUEMEZI

Onwuemezi is a writer living in London. She is the winner of The White Review Short Story Prize 2019 and her work has appeared in literary and art magazines, including *Granta, Frieze* and *Prototype*. Her debut short story collection, *Dark Neighbourhood,* was published by Fitzcarraldo Editions in 2021, and was named one of The Guardian's best books of 2021. It was shortlisted for both the Republic of Consciousness Prize and the Edge Hill Prize in 2022 and her short story *Green Afternoon* was shortlisted for the BBC National Short Story Award 2022.

KATHERINE MCKITTRICK

McKittrick is Professor of Gender Studies and Canada Research Chair in Black Studies at Queen's University in Kingston, Canada. She authored *Demonic Grounds: Black Women and the Cartographies of Struggle* (2006) and edited and contributed to *Sylvia Wynter: On Being Human as Praxis* (2015). Her most recent monograph, *Dear Science and Other Stories* (2021) is an exploration of black methodologies.

MARTINE SYMS

Syms is an artist who has earned wide recognition for a practice combining conceptual grit, humour and social commentary. She has exhibited extensively including solo exhibitions at the Museum of Modern Art, the Art Institute of Chicago and Tate Modern. Commissioned work includes brands such as Prada, Nike, Celine and NTS Radio, among others. She is a recipient of the Herb Alpert Award, the Creative Capital Award, a United States Artists fellowship, the Tiffany Foundation Award, the Future Fields Art Prize and is a 2023 Guggenheim Fellow. Syms is the writer and director of *The African Desperate* (2022), which was nominated for an Independent Spirit Award in 2023.

DANIELLA ROSE KING

King is a curator and writer. She is Adjunct Curator, Caribbean Diasporic Art, Hyundai Tate Research Centre: Transnational, and Associate Lecturer, Curating at Teesside University. She edited and contributed to *The Last Place They Thought Of* (2018) and *Deborah Anzinger: An Unlikely Birth* (2019) and her writing has appeared in *Simone Leigh* (2023), *Life Between Islands: Caribbean-British Art 1950s to Now* (2021), Whitney Biennial (2019), *Refractions: Highlights from The Studio Museum in Harlem* (2019), *Women and Performance: A Journal of Feminist Theory* (2018), *Other Cinemas: Politics, Culture and Experimental Film in the 1970s* (2017) and she is co-editor of a forthcoming anthology on Caribbean aesthetics and the Capitalocene (2024).